History of the Jews in America

History

BY DEBORAH PESSIN

ILLUSTRATIONS BY RUTH GIKOW

United Synagogue

of the Jews
in America

NEW YORK

Commission on Jewish Education

5717–1957

Third Printing

Library of Congress Catalog Card Number: 57-7421

To the Memory of
LEO L. HONOR
Teacher, Scholar, Friend
whose influence on American Jewish life
is reflected in this book

זצ״ל

PREFACE

The writing of a history book is much like the journey of Ulysses, its way beset with numerous enchantments to bedevil reason. Particularly Ulysses-wise is the writing of an American Jewish history, with its many bypaths, each with its rich blossoms, each inviting the writer to linger awhile and succumb to its allurements. Many a full-blown blossom must be by-passed, many a shy violet must be brought to view. Development in the religious area, in the educational, the economic, the cultural, the philanthropic, all must be accorded proper perspective if the picture of Jewish life in America is to be grasped in its totality.

The writer wishes to express her gratitude to those who helped her steer clear of the allurements and reach haven. She wishes to thank the United Synagogue Commission on Jewish Education and its chairman, Rabbi Josiah Derby, and the Committee on Textbook Publications and its chairman, Henry R. Goldberg. She is grateful to the readers for their many helpful suggestions, to Dr. Moshe Davis, Dr. Judah Goldin, Dr. Solomon Grayzel, A. Hillel Henkin, Hyman J. Kisch, William B. Lakritz, Reuben Reznik, Rabbi Saul Teplitz. The advice and suggestions of Rabbi Isidore E. Meyer and Barnet Cohen were particularly valuable. The writer also wishes to thank Ruth Gikow for her superb art work, and Peter Oldenburg for the creative quality of his book designing. Expressions of gratitude can scarcely define her indebtedness to her adviser, the late Dr. Leo L. Honor, and to the Educational Director of the Commission on Jewish Education, Dr. Abraham E. Millgram. Without their help, it is difficult to see how this book could have seen the light of day.

CONTENTS

UNIT THREE
Building Jewish Life

UNIT FOUR
The New Pioneers

UNIT FIVE
New Responsibilities

Sketches From American Jewish Life

INTRODUCTION

Dear Reader:

A book's introduction is meant to introduce the book to its reader. It is meant to give a short preview of what is in the book as well as a glimpse of the past, that is, of the events that led to the subject matter dealt with in the book.

But it is no easy matter to give the reader a brief glimpse into the past of the Jewish people. For never was there a people with such an amazing past, a people that began its life as a nation in a tiny land surrounded by stronger nations, was conquered again and again, and instead of vanishing from the face of the earth, saw its conquerors vanish instead. Never was there a people that withstood such dispersion, persecution and terror, and still lived to tell the tale. "A stiff-necked people," their leader Moses had once called them angrily. But perhaps it was this very stubbornness that kept them on the path they chose to follow, once they had made the choice. No bribes, no promise of a life of comfort free of persecution, no threat of torture or even death, could make them abandon the religion and customs of their fathers. And often, the greater the suffering, the more ardent became their love for their own way of life.

But retaining their past did not mean, for the Jews, living in the past. They dreamed dreams of returning to the homeland from which they had been torn. They prayed for the Messiah to come and gather them from the four corners of the world and lead them back to the distant land of their dreams. They read the books written by their sages of bygone days. They observed their laws and clung to

11

the teachings of their prophets and rabbis. Yet wherever they were permitted, they kept abreast of the times, absorbing the culture about them and contributing to it. They became statesmen, physicians, merchants, writers, philosophers, men of science and the arts. They went on voyages of discovery and charted the skies and the seas. Often they were pioneers, hacking their way through wildernesses and blazing trails for others to follow. Often they were heroes, giving all, even their lives, to preserve or build what they considered important to mankind. And as is true with all peoples, most of them were ordinary members of society, quietly earning a living, contributing, from day to day, to the development of the civilization in which they lived.

Thus it was with the Jews of America. At the same time that they preserved the way of life they had inherited from their fathers, they shared in the development of the new, freedom-loving way of life being built by their fellow Americans. Not only their talents and skills and energies, but also their ideals of freedom and justice which they had carried with them through the dark centuries of misery and persecution, went into the building of America. "History showed me," said Harry S. Truman, ". . . that what came about in Philadelphia in 1776 really had its beginning in Hebrew times."

The first group of Jews came to what is now the United States in 1654, when America still seemed a fearsome wilderness to most people in the Old World. Had Moses seen this handful of Jews, these few pioneers who had braved everything to preserve the laws he had given them, he would again have said, "a stiff-necked people." But this time there would have been no anger, no reproach in his voice, only awe and love and admiration. He had scolded their ancestors for demanding water in the wilderness, for yearning for the fleshpots of Egypt. And here they were, the descendants of those who had tried his soul, scorning water and fleshpots and safety, coming to a new wilderness, simply to be able to live the life of their fathers. Here they were, after more than two thousand years of exile and torture and massacres, hungry and gaunt, straggling onto the shore of the New World.

Many more came after that first brave group of pioneers. They came singly, in family units, in great waves, to the haven of the New World. This book is the story of how they came and why they came and what they did when they got here. And in a sense, this book is also an introduction to a greater story which is still to unfold. For the history of the Jews in this country, like the history of all the American people, covers a little more than three hundred years, a mere moment in the story of mankind. The future still stretches before us. The greatest achievements are yet to come for the builders of America, among them, the Jews.

UNIT ONE CALL OF THE NEW WORLD

1

Leaving
the Old World

Memories of Spain

It happened in Spain, in the summer of 1492.

All day they kept coming down to the sea, some in orderly procession, some in confused groups huddled together. All day they streamed out of the provinces of Spain onto the open highways, old and young, men, women and children, on foot, on donkey, in jolting carts. Some wept as they went down the roads to the sea. But for some the time for weeping was over, and their eyes were blank in faces drawn with despair.

On March 30 of that year King Ferdinand and Queen Isabella had issued the Edict of Expulsion, giving the Jews four months to dispose of their possessions and leave Spain. Leave Spain, they thought bitterly, trudging down the roads. Leave all they had built during the hundreds of years they had lived in Spain. Leave their homes, their green meadows, their lofty synagogues, their famous academies, the cemeteries sheltering the bones of their dead.

For many centuries there had been Jews in Spain. They had seen, through the years, the rise and fall of civilizations. Like the tide of

17

the Mediterranean washing back and forth on the coast of Spain, they had seen mighty armies overrun the land, then withdraw before the forces of new invaders. When the Romans, under Julius Caesar, came to the Iberian Peninsula, reaching out for more land to rule, they had found the Jews already there, and no one knew when their first pioneers had reached Spain, or how they had come. About four hundred years later, when the Roman empire was nearing its end, the Germanic warriors swept down from their rude huts in the north to seize Spain from the Romans. Among the civilized inhabitants, the new conquerors found the Jews, a people who had developed a religion, Judaism, the mother religion of Christianity and Mohammedanism, a people skilled in agriculture, in dyeing, in making glass, in trading with the lands of the East.

In the year 711 came new armies of invaders, the Mohammedans from North Africa. Mohammedans and Jews, both lovers of culture, made Spain a cultural center of Europe. Under the friendly reign of the Mohammedan rulers, the Jews of Spain developed their poetry and philosophy. Their scientists studied the stars and the waters and their physicians healed the sick. In other lands of Europe their people were forced to wear yellow badges and strange headgear to set them apart from the Christians. They were taxed into poverty, hounded from place to place, accused of poisoning wells, set upon by mobs. In Spain alone did the Jews walk in freedom, building their synagogues and academies, serving as advisers to the caliphs, sending their ships over the waters for the treasures of the Orient. For four hundred years they had lived their Golden Age in Spain.

The Last of the Mohammedans

Time passed, and the Mohammedans, grown unaccustomed to warfare, were forced to yield to the Christian armies that invaded Spain. Province by province, Spain fell into the hands of new rulers.

At first the Jews continued to live as they had in the past. But gradually, the persecution the Jews suffered in other lands overtook them in Spain.

Early Christians and Jews had once been friendly enough. But as Christianity began to spread, many church leaders, wishing Christianity to become the universal religion, had tried to draw the Jews into its fold. They tried persuasion, and when that failed, they tried force. They slandered the Jews to the simple-minded peasants and town dwellers, planting in their minds the seeds of fear and hatred. Was a peasant so poor that he could not feed himself properly? It was not the rich lord of the manor who oppressed him, but the Jew, the peasant was told, who was to blame. Had a man's wife and children died at the time of the Black Death that raged over the continent of Europe? It was the Jews, it was whispered, who had poisoned the wells. Gradually, the Jews became the scapegoat of the Christian world, blamed for all its ills, for the poverty of the peasants, for the diseases that ravaged the populations.

It was in January, 1492, that Granada, the last of the strongholds of the Mohammedans, passed into the hands of Ferdinand and Isabella. The Mohammedan ruler of Granada gazed for the last time on his golden-domed Alhambra, the fortress palace his fathers had built, and burst into tears. Then he departed, and Ferdinand and Isabella, accompanied by ringing bells and the wild cheers of their victorious armies, entered the Alhambra.

The Inquisition

Three months later, on March 30, came the decree that all the Jews must be out of Spain by August. For the king and queen had been persuaded by Torquemada, master of the Inquisition, that this was the only way to have a united, Christian Spain. The Church had tried in every way to convert the Jews to Christianity. To escape persecution and death, many Jews had let themselves be baptized.

But the Marranos, as the baptized Jews were called, were often suspected of practicing Jewish customs in the secrecy of their homes. Torquemada had then set up the Inquisition, and in its chambers the suspected Marranos were tried for disloyalty to Christianity. They were tortured into confession that they had eaten *matzah* on Passover, or had fasted on Yom Kippur. Thousands of Marranos spent their last days in the dungeons of the Inquisition, and thousands were burned alive in the fires of the *autos-da-fé*.

At last a thought came to Torquemada. If there were men and women living openly as Jews, observing their Jewish customs as they chose, would they not always serve as examples to the Marranos and encourage them in their secret practices? If Spain was to be all Christian, thought Torquemada, would it not be best to get rid of the Jews?

Torquemada went to Ferdinand and Isabella with his plan to expel the Jews. But the monarchs hesitated. Much of Spain's glory would depart with the Jews. For there were many scientists among them, men of medicine, merchants, valuable advisers. On the other hand, they would be unable to take all their possessions with them. Their wealth, like that of the Marranos condemned by the Inquisition, would fall to the royal treasury. The war with the Mohammedans had been costly. Gold was needed for many things, gold to fill the royal coffers, gold to pay for the wars.

Exile

The Edict of Expulsion was signed and the exodus began. But thousands of Jews lingered, hoping that some miracle would save them. Through April they waited, through May, June, July. Isaac Abrabanel, financial adviser to the king and queen, pleaded for his people, offering vast sums of money if the Jews could remain. But his pleading was in vain, so effectively had Torquemada done his work. And Isaac Abrabanel, a scholarly old man who stemmed, it

was said, from the House of David, prepared for the road of exile with his people.

"Let us surmount every obstacle for the honor of our nation and our religion . . ." he appealed to his grieving people. "If they leave us with life, we will live; if they deprive us of it, we will die; but never let us violate our Holy Law."

In the frantic days before their departure, they had wept and prayed in the synagogues which would no longer be theirs. They had sold what they could of their possessions, a house for a donkey, a vineyard for a stout pair of shoes. It was on August 2, which fell on Tishah B'Av, the day of mourning for the Temple which had been destroyed in Jerusalem, that the last of the three hundred thousand Jews made their way out of the provinces of Spain. All day they stumbled along the highways to the sea, clutching family heirlooms, old family Bibles, stones taken from the cemeteries inscribed with the names of their dead. All day they streamed out of the land that had been home for hundreds of years.

The Discoverer

That same day, on August 2, Christopher Columbus sailed out of the harbor of Palos, passing several ships crowded with Jews exiled from Spain. A fine mist rose over the waters as Columbus' three vessels skimmed over the waves, and white seagulls circled and dipped overhead. At the helm of the flagship, the *Santa Maria*, Columbus stood, his hair grown gray through the long years of waiting.

For Columbus had waited long for the three small vessels to carry him and his crew to the west. He had gone first to the king of

Portugal with his plan to find a short route to the Indies. But the wise men of Portugal had told the king it was not possible, and Columbus had gone to Spain. He had waited in Spain for seven years, while Ferdinand and Isabella had hurled their armies against the fortresses of Granada. He had begged them to outfit a small expedition, a crew of sailors and several vessels. In return, he had promised to find the riches of the East by a short route, the spices, silks, ivory, rugs, damask, gems, perfumes, porcelain, the treasures of the Orient so highly prized in the markets of Europe.

But like the king of Portugal, Ferdinand and Isabella had paid little attention to their petitioner. At last, despairing of ever finding help in Spain, Columbus had mounted his donkey and had started for France. Perhaps, he thought, the king of France would listen. Perhaps in France he would find the support the Portuguese and Spanish monarchs had denied him.

As Columbus jogged along the road, several men pleaded with the Spanish monarchs to recall him before it was too late. There was Gabriel Sanchez, a Marrano, treasurer of the kingdom. There was Luis de Santangel, a Marrano, chancellor of the royal household. And since this took place several months before the expulsion, it was not too late for Don Isaac Abrabanel to add his pleas to those of Gabriel Sanchez and Luis de Santangel.

But the royal house, said Isabella, had no money, since the long

wars with the Mohammedans had drained the treasury. It did not matter, said Luis de Santangel. He would advance seventeen thousand florins to help outfit an expedition.

Then a messenger was sent to bring Columbus back to the court. And on August 2, the day the last of the Jews had departed from Spain, Columbus sailed out of Palos. "Having banished all the Jews from all your kingdoms," he wrote in his diary, "you ordered me to go to India."

The Mystery of Columbus

There are some historians who believe that Columbus was a Marrano, a secret Jew. If he were not a Jew, they say, why was he so secretive about his parents and the place of his birth? For there are fourteen cities claiming the honor of being Columbus' birthplace. And, the scholars ask, why was he drawn to Jews and Marranos, sending the first reports of his voyage to Gabriel Sanchez and Luis de Santangel? And why did he make notes in his diary of the plight of the Jews, first of their expulsion, and later of his having passed the ships bearing them from Spain? Did he, the historians ask, feel bound to a people he did not dare claim openly as his own? And if Columbus was Italian, and not a Spanish Marrano, why did he use Spanish and not Italian in his diary and letters? Is it not probable, these historians go on, that his family fled from their native Spain and went to Italy to live, where they would be safe from the Inquisition?

Most of the historians and scholars, however, have not accepted the theory that Columbus was a Jew, or of Jewish descent.

Sailing West

Out of Palos and over the waters of the Sea of Darkness Columbus sailed, taking with him the secret of his birth, and taking with

him five Marranos, Alonso de la Calle, Rodrigo Sanchez, relative
of Gabriel Sanchez, Bernal and Marco, physicians, and Luis de
Torres, to serve as his interpreter.

Believing that Columbus was a madman, few sailors were willing
to risk their lives on the dangerous voyage. To complete the crew,
a number of prisoners, *degradados,* were released from prison and
forced to sail with Columbus. Among the *degradados,* some historians believe, there may have been Marranos.

The nautical knowledge and inventions of Jews, too, went with
Columbus. The discoverer took with him "Jacob's Staff," a sea
quadrant invented by Levi ben Gerson to study the position of the
stars. In the isolation of his cabin, Columbus pored over the astro-
nomical tables and almanacs of Abraham Zacuto, and studied the
famous maps of Judah Cresques, the "map Jew."

The shoreline of Spain slowly receded, merging with the waters.
On the *Nina,* the *Pinta* and the *Santa Maria,* the sailors fell to their

Section of Map by Judah Cresques

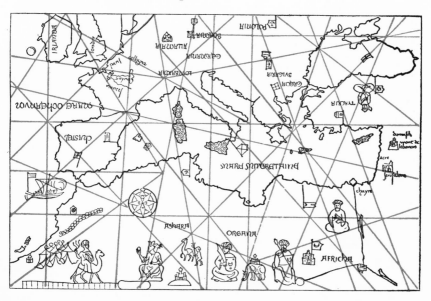

knees and wept and prayed, for they believed they would never
return. They remembered the stories they had heard, stories of mon-
sters who swallowed ships whole, and of boiling waters where they
might burn to a crisp, and of the giant squid, which pulled ships
down to their destruction at the bottom of the sea. If they managed
to escape these, they thought, would they not in time reach the end
of the waters and fall into bottomless depths? Columbus, they
knew, did not believe there was an end. He believed, like many
scientists of his day, that the earth was round. But even if the scientists were right and the earth was round, how would they ever sur-
vive the long voyage over thousands of miles of water?

The days passed, and the weeks. August went by, and then September. Some of the Jews who had left Spain had by this time found
homes in Holland, where others of their people had found refuge
before them. Some had found homes in Turkey, some in Portugal,
in Italy. Many had been robbed by the captains of the vessels on
which they had sailed and left to die on desert islands.

On the Sea of Darkness, Columbus' ships still sailed westward,
into the unknown. The sailors grew restless, for they saw only endless waters reaching to the endless skies. Pacing his cabin, Columbus thought of the gems Marco Polo had brought back from the
kingdom of the Khan, the rubies and sapphires, the diamonds and
emeralds. He thought of the palace of the Khan which Marco Polo
had seen, with its halls of gold and its walls of jewelled panels. He
too, thought Columbus, would find the kingdom and the palace of
the Khan. Not by going over land by caravan as Marco Polo had
done, but by going west, over the Sea of Darkness, where no other
navigator was prepared to go.

September rolled into October. Day by day the food grew scarcer.
Parched, gaunt, desperate for dry land, the sailors scanned the
waters. Their inflamed eyes saw only waves reaching in every
direction.

The Light

On October 10 they came to their commander. They pleaded with him, begging him to turn back before they were all destroyed. But Columbus asked them to wait a little longer. Soon, he promised them, there would be land.

That night, at ten o'clock, walking the silent deck, Columbus sighted a light in the distance, like a candle rising and falling.

Out of the dark night had come the first flicker of light, the light of a bright new world.

Things to Read

Levinger, Elma Ehrlich, *The Golden Door,* Bloch Publishing Co., New York, "A Friend at Court," pp. 1-5; "In the Night Watches," pp. 6-9.

Lurie, Rose G., *The Great March,* Book Two, Union of American Hebrew Congregations, Cincinnati, "Across the Sea," pp. 4-12; "Land at Last," pp. 13-18.

Read up on the history of the Jews in Spain. Consult with your teacher or your librarian for material on this subject.

Questions to Discuss

What were the conditions in Spain that made it possible for the Jews to develop their Golden Age?

Why is it said that Judaism is the mother religion of Christianity and Mohammedanism? What principles of Judaism were adopted by Christianity and Mohammedanism?

Why did Isaac Abrabanel feel that exile was preferable to abandoning the faith of his fathers?

Things to Do

Pretend that one of the *degradados* in Columbus' crew was a Marrano. Write his story, as he might have written it. Tell about his adventures during the journey across the Sea of Darkness, about his return home to Spain. As your study of Jewish history in America continues, you may want to go on with the adventures of your hero, making the story an exciting serial with a happy ending in the New World.

Plan a large world map which will show the migrations of the Jews to America. Begin with the migration of the Jews from Spain to Portugal, Holland, Turkey. From these lands, many of them will later come to America. Continue your map work as your study progresses. Animate your map.

There are many films and records available to supplement your study of the Jews in America. We will refer you to places to write to for this material as we go along. Before sending for material, it would be best to write to the distributors for information on the price, and on other material available. Write to Eternal Light, Jewish Theological Seminary, 3080 Broadway, New York City, for information on the Eternal Light recordings.

Teachers Bibliography

Friedman, Lee M., *Jewish Pioneers and Patriots,* Jewish Publication Society, Philadelphia, 1942, "Was Christopher Columbus a Jew?" pp. 67-73.

Learsi, Rufus, *The Jews in America: A History,* World Publishing Company, New York, 1954, pp. 3-11.

Lebeson, Anita, *Pilgrim People,* Harper and Brothers, New York, 1950, pp. 1-34.

Minkin, Jacob S., *Abrabanel and the Expulsion of the Jews From Spain,* Behrman House, New York, 1954.

Kayserling, M., *Christopher Columbus and the Participation of the Jews in the Spanish and Portuguese Discoveries,* translated by C. Gross, Longmans, Green and Company, New York, 1894.

CHAPTER 2

First Jewish Settlers
in the New World

At the Edge of the New World

Columbus did not know, when he planted the flag of Spain on the island he named San Salvador, that he was at the edge of a new world. From San Salvador, Columbus sailed on till he came to Cuba. Believing that he had reached the mainland of Asia, he called two of his men, Rodrigo de Jerez and Luis de Torres, his Marrano interpreter. To Luis de Torres, Columbus entrusted a letter, written in Latin and sent by Ferdinand and Isabella to give to the Khan. Then he dispatched the men to find the palace of the mighty ruler of whom Marco Polo had told so many wonderful tales.

With two copper-skinned natives to act as their guides, Luis de Torres and Rodrigo de Jerez made their way inland, while Columbus and his crew waited for their return. In six days the men came back and the sailors gathered about them, eager for tales of the wonders they had seen.

But the stories they heard were not of palaces and heaps of priceless gems, for Luis and Rodrigo had not found the Khan's palace. The guides had taken the two white men to a small village, and

Luis de Torres, who knew Hebrew and Arabic, had spoken to the men and women of the village first in one language and then in the other, asking them how to reach the palace of the Khan. The people had been friendly, although they had not understood a word Luis de Torres had spoken. They had stared curiously at the white-skinned strangers and had shown them their village. They lived simply, in huts, Luis and Rodrigo told the crew, and they slept in hammocks or on mats woven by the women. As the crew hung on his

words, Luis de Torres described a strange custom he and Rodrigo
had observed. The natives smoked leaves rolled up into cylinders.
A man would put one end of the rolled up leaves, which they called
tabacos, into his mouth. He lighted the other end, making it look
like a brand. Then he puffed on the *tabacos,* while smoke came out
of his mouth and nose.

Columbus continued his search for the palace of the Khan, cruis-
ing in and out among the small islands. At last, still believing that
he had reached Asia, Columbus returned to Spain, planning to
come again with a larger expedition.

One man, however, did not return with Columbus. Luis de Torres
preferred to remain with the friendly, copper-skinned natives who
did not ask him how he worshipped, and who had never heard of
the Inquisition and *autos-da-fé*. Enjoying a royal pension from the
monarchs of Spain, Luis de Torres spent the rest of his life in Cuba,
the first Marrano to settle in the New World.

Coming of the White Man

Twice again Columbus came back over the Sea of Darkness, and
still he did not realize that he had found a new world. After Columbus' death, Amerigo Vespucci, an Italian navigator employed
by Spain, continued the search for a western route to the Indies.
Vespucci hit upon the eastern shore of what is now called South
America. When he returned home, he wrote to his friends that he
believed he had found a new world.

More and more navigators now followed in the tracks of Columbus and Vespucci. With the return of each vessel, new tales were
spread about the wonders and the beauty of the New World. Explorers told of jungles and tempestuous rivers, of lithe, copper-
skinned men who made their way over waterways in light canoes
and who used only bows and arrows to defend themselves. They
told of gold and silver, and of chattering monkeys and bright-col-

ored peacocks and parrots inhabiting the thick jungles undisturbed by man.

The rulers of Spain and Portugal, eager for wealth and power, sent explorei and soldiers to the New World to find precious metal and gems ar to seize the land from the natives. Sent by the rulers of Spain, Cortez discovered Mexico, a rich, fertile land which was ruled by Mc ezuma. Cortez did not find it difficult to conquer the friendly people who had trusted him, and who were unequal to the Spanish conquerors in methods of warfare. As Cortez did in Mexico, Pizarro, another Spaniard, did in Peru. He overcame the natives, conquered the land, and looted the temples, the palaces, even the tombs, of their gold and silver and gems.

From Spain, then from Portugal too, came more and more vessels to the countries which are now called Central and South America. Some men came as conquerors, to seize land and to grow rich on the gold and silver and precious stones they took from the natives. Some came to find adventure beyond the jungles and the rushing streams. But there were some who came neither for riches nor for adventure. They came to find freedom in the New World.

Marranos in the New World

Many of the Jews driven from Spain had gone to Portugal, where King John had permitted them to remain for a time on condition that they pay eight *crusados* for each refugee. But when the daughter of Ferdinand and Isabella refused to marry Manuel, son of the king of Portugal, unless the "infidels" were banished, the Jews and Mohammedans were given ten months to become Christians.

For the Marranos of Spain and Portugal, the New World held a promise of freedom. Was it not possible, they thought, that on the great continent, removed by thousands of miles of water from Spain and Portugal, they could at last free themselves of their persecutors and openly worship in the way of their fathers? In the

fresh, green world across the ocean, could they not escape the Inquisition that had taken the lives of so many of their people?

Marranos came with the first pioneers to the New World. They settled on the islands of the West Indies, in Brazil, in Mexico. Some of them, unable to cope with the unbearable heat and the primitive conditions on the edge of the jungle, died of tropical diseases. But vessels kept arriving from Spain and Portugal bringing new Marrano settlers who were willing to brave the dangers of the heat and the jungles so that they could find freedom in the New World.

Gradually, large tracts of forestland were cleared and the jungle was beaten back. In Brazil, which was ruled by Portugal, Marranos imported sugar cane from Madeira and cultivated their own sugar plantations. Because they had friends in Spain, Portugal and Holland, they were able to send them products of the New World—sugar, tobacco, peacocks, apes, furs—to sell in the markets of the Old World. Often, when the vessels returned, they brought human cargo, more Marranos eager to live in freedom.

But though many miles of ocean stretched between the two worlds, the Marrano pioneers were unable to escape the Inquisition. The vessels sent by Spain and Portugal with new settlers for their colonies also brought priests to convert the natives to Christianity and to keep an eye on the Marranos. Marranos in Portuguese colonies suspected of loyalty to Judaism were sent back to Portugal, where the Inquisition had by this time been set up. And because so many Marranos had fled from Spain to the New World, Spain set up a branch of the Inquisition on American soil. Hundreds of Marranos in Mexico were burned at the stake while Indian natives witnessed with amazement the cruelty of their white conquerors.

The Rise of Holland

Spain and Portugal could not long remain the sole possessors of the New World. Pope Alexander VI had drawn an imaginary line dividing the world in two, half for Spain and half for Portugal. But England, France and Holland did not accept the Pope's division. They too wanted a share of the riches that had been discovered in the west.

Holland had lagged far behind in the race for land across the sea. In the middle of the sixteenth century, Holland had become subject to King Philip II of Spain. When King Philip tried to uproot the Protestant religion in Holland, bringing in the Inquisition, the little country, under William of Orange, had revolted. War raged for many years between the small land of dikes and the land of the Inquisition. Finally all the provinces of the Netherlands united to throw off their foreign rulers and gain their independence. When the war was over and freedom won, Holland tried to make up for the time lost. Dutch merchants, searching for new markets for their goods, founded the Dutch West India Company and cast longing eyes on the New World.

The Coming of the Dutch

The Dutch West India Company wanted to gain a foothold in South America. Studying its coastline and the reports of returning sea captains, they learned about a beautiful harbor city called Recife. Recife, the "City of Reefs," perched on a peninsula among tropical fruit trees. Because of its position on the peninsula and its two miles of natural harbor, it had grown into the most important city of Portuguese Brazil. At the outskirts of the city lay wide plantations, many of them owned by Marranos, which produced valuable sugar and tobacco. The Marranos had also set up sugar mills and warehouses for their goods, and the center of the city had little shops filled with domestic and foreign goods.

The Jews, the Dutch West India Company knew, were friendly to the Dutch, for Jews had long found Holland a place of refuge where they could worship as they pleased. Jews had prospered in Holland, some of them trading with foreign lands. There were also Jews among the stockholders of the Dutch West India Company. If the Dutch were to attack Recife, which was not strongly fortified, the Marranos in the city, the Dutch West India Company believed, would help them take it from the Portuguese.

In 1630 the Dutch invaded and took the city of Recife. The Marranos joyfully celebrated the coming of the friendly Dutchmen. No longer would spies of the Inquisition dog their steps, observing what they ate, whom they spoke to, whether they observed the Sabbath. With the Dutch as rulers of Recife, they could live openly as Jews, celebrating their festivals without fear, even opening houses of worship.

Jews and Marranos came flocking to Recife from nearby cities and settlements, as well as from Spanish colonies. They came from Holland, Poland, Hungary, from the Germanic lands. The harbor city soon had so many Jews that people called it the Port of the Jews, and its main street, lined with little merchant shops, was called the Street of the Jews. Two synagogues were opened in Recife, and Dutch rabbis, bringing with them more Jewish settlers, came to the bustling harbor city of Brazil.

Fall of Recife

But Recife did not remain in Dutch hands for long. Nine years after it was conquered by the Dutch, the Portuguese returned and laid siege to the city. Jews and Dutchmen fought their enemies grimly. Holland, engaged in a war with England, was unable to send help. Food in the beleaguered city ran low, and as the weeks and months went by, people began to live on crusts of bread, and half-starved soldiers fell at their posts. Rabbi Isaac Aboab de Fonseca went among the soldiers, encouraging them to hold out. The Jews in Holland, knowing the fate that awaited their friends and relatives in Recife if they were taken by the Portuguese, called upon the government, the States General, to demand equal treatment for Dutch and Jewish prisoners of war. But the request of the States General for equal treatment of prisoners was ignored by the Portuguese invaders. The Jewish war prisoners, separated from the Dutch, were given no quarter. Some were killed, others were handed over to the Inquisition.

Finally, realizing that Recife was doomed, the Dutch command agreed to an amnesty, exacting a promise from the Portuguese commander that he would not molest the Jews. In January, 1654, the commander of the Portuguese forces, Francisco Barreto, triumphantly entered Recife. The commander did not mistreat the Jews. Instead he gave them a choice, baptism or exile. If they chose to leave Recife, they would have ninety days to dispose of their possessions.

The Jews chose to leave Recife. They sold what they could to their neighbors, their mills, their stores, their homes and plantations. And leaving the city of white beaches and gardens of lemon and pomegranate trees, they dispersed in every direction. Hundreds returned to Holland. Some scattered through Central America. Some fled to the islands of the West Indies.

Twenty-three found their way to North America, the first group of Jews to come to the land we now call the United States.

Things to Read

Leonard, Oscar, *Americans All,* Behrman House, New York, 1944,
  "Jews Helped Too," pp. 5-28.
Pessin, Deborah, *Giants on the Earth,* Behrman House, New York, 1940,
  "Sail On, O My People," pp. 1-10.

Questions to Discuss

How did the freedom the Jews enjoyed under the Dutch in Brazil affect
  the economic development of the country?
Why did many Jews leave their safe haven in Holland to come to Brazil?

Things to Do

Continue with your map showing the migrations of the Jews to the New
  World. To animate your map, first do some research on the sailing
  vessels used, on the clothes worn, on the flora and fauna of Brazil.
Some of the Jews who came to Mexico fled inland to escape the spies of
  the Inquisition. Living among the Indians for many generations, they
  came to look like the Indians, though they still retained their own
  religion. Write the story, or diary, of one of the Jewish Indians of
  Mexico. You may want to do some research before you write your
  story.

Teachers Bibliography

Friedman, Lee M., *Jewish Pioneers and Patriots,* "The Martyrdom of
  Francisco Maldonado de Silva," pp. 73-80.
Learsi, Rufus, *The Jews in America,* pp. 35-56.
Lebeson, Anita, *Pilgrim People,* pp. 35-56.
Marcus, Jacob Rader, *Early American Jewry,* Volume One, Jewish
  Publication Society, Philadelphia, 1951, pp. 3-24.

CHAPTER **3**

Settling in New Amsterdam

The Sighting of a Ship

One day in September, in the year 1654, the flag went up in the fort of New Amsterdam on the tip of the Island of Manhattan. As the flag fluttered in the breeze, men, women and children came streaming to the wharf, for a raised flag meant that a ship had been sighted, usually a ship from Holland. Several merchants in baggy pantaloons, followed by a small group of Indians, came out of the warehouse and joined the crowd at the wharf. The Indians had brought beaver skins to sell, but they were content to interrupt the bargaining till the vessel docked.

A vessel from Holland meant letters from the homeland and goods for the homes of New Amsterdam. The housewives, gazing out at the vessel that bobbed like a cork on the waters, thought comfortably of spinning wheels, carved oaken chests to hold their linens, white and blue tiles painted with biblical scenes to set around their fireplaces, tulip bulbs for their gardens. The children thought of ice skates, for the days were growing shorter and soon winter would come, and the water of the creek would freeze to a smooth glossy surface. If there were sleds in the cargo, they could go coasting down Beaver's Path.

Stubborn Peter

At a window of his large stone house not far from the water's edge, Peter Stuyvesant, Governor of the colony, also stood waiting for the vessel to sail into harbor. As he waited, his eyes roved over the crowd and a frown creased his brow. He knew that if he appeared among these people whom he governed and waited with them, the chattering and laughter would dissolve like smoke in the wind. For the people stood in awe of Peter Stuyvesant, and some of them did not approve of his harsh, stern measures. They would not show disrespect to their Governor, but their ease would vanish and the men would stiffen, as though about to receive orders.

"Old Silverleg," he had heard the children whisper behind his back. "Stubborn Pete," others called him. It was a good thing to be stubborn, the Governor believed, or the colony would fall apart. Quakers, Baptists, Presbyterians had drifted into New Amsterdam from the English colonies, but Stuyvesant had asked them to leave. New Amsterdam, he believed, should be only for those who worshipped as he did. One Quaker had insisted on preaching, though Peter Stuyvesant had warned him. To put an end to it, the Governor had had the Quaker tied to a cart and dragged over the road to the ferry. Stuyvesant's own people had at last taken the part of the Quaker, insisting that the persecution stop. Peter Stuyvesant set his lips grimly. He could not let anyone who wished come to New Amsterdam. Only a few weeks ago a Jew, Jacob Barsimson, had come from Holland on the *Peartree*. It was well that Barsimson did not bring a family or friends, thought Peter Stuyvesant. One Jew or two, he reflected, could not contaminate a colony of a thousand.

The Arrival

As the vessel came close enough for the Dutch settlers to see its colors, a murmur of disappointment passed through the crowd. There would be no letters from home, no oaken chests or tulip bulbs or spinning wheels. For it was not a Dutch sailing vessel that came into port that September day in 1654. It was a French man-of-war, a frigate armed with cannon, and its cargo was twenty-three Jews who had fled from Recife.

They watched silently as the passengers disembarked and came ashore. The new arrivals, who carried only a few bundles of clothes and some household goods, looked thin and haggard, though their faces were still burnished with the hot, southern sun. After them came several sailors, carrying iron-bound chests which they set down beside the group of refugees. The sailors, soon followed by their mates, sauntered off in search of a tavern, leaving the group alone with the Dutch settlers.

"Welkom!" one of the Dutchmen called out cheerily.

"Welkom! Welkom!" several others took up the greeting.

"Waar kom jelui vandaan?" a woman asked. "Where do you come from?"

Asser Levy, one of the passengers who seemed bolder than the rest, explained that they were Jews, from Recife, which had been taken by the Portuguese.

The settlers were disturbed by the bad news. They knew that the Dutch and the Portuguese had been fighting in Brazil, but they had not heard that Recife had fallen. What of the Dutch possessions of Surinam and Curaçao in the Caribbean area, they asked Asser Levy. Had they been taken too? They were still in Dutch hands, Asser Levy reassured them. In fact, some of the Jews from Recife had fled to Dutch territory.

And how did one make a living in New Amsterdam, several of the new arrivals asked. There were a number of things one might do. A man could hire himself out to a farmer, or a baker, or an artisan. But the most profitable occupation in New Amsterdam was buying furs from the Indians. A Dutch merchant, taking his thin-stemmed pipe from his mouth, explained that a beaver pelt was worth from four to eight *guilders,* depending on its condition. The pelts were shipped to Holland in exchange for products the settlers could not get in the New World—furniture, spinning wheels, Delft china, pewterware, velvets, calico, ornaments, boots, and many other things.

The captain of the French vessel, the *St. Catherine,* came ashore, carrying the ship papers rolled up under his arm. He called to Asser Levy, who detached himself from the group with several other men to follow the captain. Captain Jacques de la Motthe, who had stopped off at New Amsterdam many times before, led Asser Levy and his friends over the cobbled streets where geese honked and dogs barked, to the *Stadt-Huys,* the courthouse of New Amsterdam. For the French captain had a claim against his passengers. They had promised to pay him two-thousand, five-hundred *guilders* for their passage, and they had paid him only nine-hundred and thirty-three. The passengers had assured the captain that they would pay him the rest when they received help from their friends in Holland. But Jacques de la Motthe wanted the council members to know that the refugees were his debtors, and that he had first claim on anything they received.

While the matter was being discussed in the *Stadt-Huys,* the passengers arranged with the Dutch settlers for temporary homes. One man offered his attic, another the backroom of his shop. A woman offered a room in her house. Her husband and son had sailed up the Henry Hudson River (the North River, she called it) to trade at Fort Orange, and they would not be back for several months.

The Auction

The great brazen bell of the *Stadt-Huys* rang out over New Amsterdam. Its heavy clang reverberated over the streets lined with gable-roofed houses, over the hill where the windmill moved its giant arms in the autumn breeze, through the fields beyond the town where tow-headed children gathered wild carrots to bring home to their mothers. Like the raising of the flag in the fort, the clanging of the bell held a promise of some unusual event in the Dutch colony, and the settlers came hurrying to see what it could be. Perhaps Peter Stuyvesant had an important announcement to

make, or perhaps there had been an unfortunate incident between the Dutch traders and the Swedes, who had a colony on the Delaware River.

But Peter Stuyvesant had no orders to give the people, nor had there been trouble with the Swedes. It was to announce an auction sale that the bell was ringing. The Dutch magistrates had decided that in order to pay Jacques de la Motthe the money they owed him, the Jews must sell the goods they had brought with them at public auction, and the proceeds of the sale were to be turned over to the French captain. There was not much the refugees had to sell, but there were a few good pieces of pewter, a few shining pots and pans. The objects held up for sale were soon disposed of, and the townspeople returned over the cobbled streets to their homes.

But still there was not enough money to make up the sum the refugees owed the captain. The magistrates decided that Moses Ambrosius and David Israel must go to prison till the debt was paid.

Several days later, they decided that Asser Levy too was to be held in prison. But in time the prisoners were released, and as soon as they were able, they paid the captain for their passage to New Amsterdam.

A Letter for Peter Stuyvesant

In the meantime, Peter Stuyvesant had written to his employers, the Dutch West India Company. Twenty-three poor Jews had come to New Amsterdam, he complained. He had asked them to leave, but they had refused. He now awaited permission from the directors of the Dutch West India Company to expel them from New Amsterdam.

But the Jews in New Amsterdam had also written to Holland. They described their plight to their friends in Amsterdam, and the unfriendliness of Peter Stuyvesant.

The leaders of the Jews of Amsterdam lost no time in appealing to the Dutch West India Company. They pointed out how bravely their people had fought in Brazil when Recife was attacked by the Portuguese. "Yonder land is extensive and spacious," said the petition, and the more of loyal people that came to live there, the richer and greater the Dutch settlement would become.

In the spring of 1655, seven months after the twenty-three Jews came to New Amsterdam, the flag went up in the fort, bringing the settlers flocking to the wharf. A ship from Holland sailed into port, bearing a letter for Peter Stuyvesant from the Dutch West India Company. The Jews, said the letter, were to remain, provided they took care of their own poor.

The Struggle for Rights

The Jews of New Amsterdam soon grew accustomed to life in the Dutch settlement. They found homes and made friends with their neighbors and with the Indians. The men learned how to manage fishing skiffs and long Indian canoes. The women learned how to sand their floors as the Dutch women did, and what vegetables to plant in their gardens.

Grudgingly, the Governor and his Council of Nine Men yielded to the demands of the Jews for more and more rights. Sometimes the Governor did not yield till he was rebuked by his employers in Holland, and sometimes he yielded before the matter was brought before the Dutch West India Company. Peter Stuyvesant did not want the Jews to go to Fort Orange, on the Hudson River, or down the Delaware River to trade. When one of the Jews tried to buy himself a house, the Governor and the Council of Nine objected again. But "Stubborn Peter" received a sharp letter from the Dutch West India Company ordering him to permit the Jews to buy real estate and to trade with the Indians.

In August, 1655, Peter Stuyvesant was busy organizing an expedition to fight the Swedes in New Sweden, on the Delaware River. Seven hundred men were enlisted for the expedition to capture the Swedish fort. To guard the Dutch colony against possible Indian attack while he was away, Stuyvesant enlisted men to mount guard at home. The Jews, he decided, were not to be permitted to serve as guards. Instead, every able-bodied Jew between the age of sixteen and sixty was to pay a tax.

Jacob Barsimson and Asser Levy appeared at the *Stadt-Huys* to speak to the Governor and his Council. They wanted to mount guard like everyone else, they said. But the Governor and his Council shrugged their shoulders. If the Jews did not like the ruling, they declared, they were free to go elsewhere to live.

But the Jews did not wish to go elsewhere. They remained in New Amsterdam, fighting for their rights. In time, the ruling was dropped. Jacob Barsimson, Asser Levy, and other able-bodied Jews took their turn standing guard to protect the colony against attack.

Two years later, Asser Levy, who had grown more prosperous, again appeared at the *Stadt-Huys*. He wanted the rights and privileges of all burghers, said Asser Levy. And he pulled a paper from his pocket and held it out for the Council to see. The paper was a certificate from Amsterdam, where he had once lived, showing that Asser Levy had been a burgher of the city, enjoying the rights and privileges of all Dutchmen. But the Governor and his Council refused to give a Jew the rights of all burghers, and Asser Levy's appeal was denied.

Asser Levy withdrew, but his fight was not over. Now four other Jews came to the *Stadt-Huys*. They spoke strongly to the irate Governor and his Council. They pointed out that Jews had stood guard. They had paid their taxes, had contributed to strengthening the outer wall of the city. They had done all that loyal citizens were required to do. They had been upheld time and again by the Dutch West India Company. Now they demanded for themselves, as well as for all the Jews, the right of free citizenship.

Neither the stubbornness nor the iron will of the Governor prevailed. More Jews came to New Amsterdam from Holland and from the West Indies, and together with the earlier arrivals, they won their battle for citizenship. But there were several rights the Jews in New Amsterdam could not win, the right to open retail shops, the right to practice the crafts, and the right to have a public house of worship. It was not till after 1664, when New Amsterdam was captured by the English and became New York, that these rights were gradually won.

Building Their Inner Life

While the Jewish settlers of New Amsterdam fought for the rights of burghers, they also insisted on following their own way of life. They had braved the horrors of the Inquisition in Spain and Portugal, or the nightmare of exile, because they had refused to give up the religion and customs of their fathers. They had taken the perilous voyage across miles of ocean to live in the disease-ridden wilderness of Brazil, hoping to find freedom in the New World. They had built their homes and hewn out their plantations and planted their gardens, when again they were given the choice, this time by Francisco Barreto, of baptism or exile. Weary of persecution, weary of seeking homes and security, they might have taken the easier way. They might have chosen to be baptized so that their wanderings would at last be over. But again they chose exile, preferring the weary search for new homes to giving up their own way of life.

In New Amsterdam they were confronted by a prejudiced governor. But the small group of Jews who had sacrificed all they had to find freedom in some corner of the world were not easily intimidated by Peter Stuyvesant. Peter Stuyvesant prevented them from having a synagogue, but he could not prevent them from observing their Sabbath and their festivals, nor from meeting in their own homes for prayer. Important to the Jewish settlers was the kind of

food they ate. They wanted *kosher* meat, the fowl and cattle slaughtered according to the Jewish regulations. Since there were no Jewish butchers in New Amsterdam, Asser Levy soon filled the need. Building his slaughterhouse on what today is Wall Street, he sold meat, and probably served as *shoḥet,* ritual slaughterer, for the Jewish group. For according to the records, Asser Levy was excused from killing hogs, a meat forbidden to Jews.

"Giving them liberty," Peter Stuyvesant had complained to the Dutch West India Company, "we cannot refuse the Lutherans and Papists." Peter Stuyvesant was right. In insisting on their own civil rights and on maintaining their own way of life, the Jews helped establish liberty for other minorities in New Amsterdam.

Things to Read

Blandford, Benjamin W., *Off the Capes of Delaware,* Union of American Hebrew Congregations, Cincinnati, 1940, "Adventures of Jacob Barsimson," pp. 62-77.

Levinger, Elma Ehrlich, *The Golden Door,* "When Katrina Lost Her Way," pp. 10-25; "The Jew Who Would Not Pay," pp. 26-35.

Spitz, Leon, *What the Liberty Bell Proclaimed,* National Women's League of the United Synagogue of America, New York, 1951, "Two Purim Nights," pp. 11-16; "Night Watch," pp. 17-25.

Questions to Discuss

Why was it unnecessary for the Dutch West India Company to stipulate that the Jews could remain in New Amsterdam provided they took care of their own poor? Can you point to Jewish customs and laws which require that Jews take care of their poor?

How, in insisting on their own rights, did the Jews of New Amsterdam help build freedom for other minorities?

Things to Do

Write to the Commission on Jewish Education, Union of American Hebrew Congregations, 838 Fifth Avenue, New York 21, N. Y. for the filmstrip, "The Jews Settle in New Amsterdam—1654."

Pretend you are Asser Levy. Write a letter to a friend in Holland telling him about the last days in Recife and about life in New Amsterdam.

Teachers Bibliography

Friedman, Lee M., *Jewish Pioneers and Patriots,* "Asser Levy Van Swellem," pp. 133-140.

Learsi, Rufus, *The Jews in America,* pp. 26-31.

Marcus, Jacob Rader, *Early American Jewry,* Volume One, pp. 24-33.

Pool, David de Sola, *Portraits Etched in Stone,* Columbia University Press, New York, 1952.

CHAPTER 4

Homes in
Rhode Island

The First English Colonies

The builders of America came slowly at first. For many, the voyage was too costly. And it was still dangerous to cross the sea in the small vessels which had been built for coastal voyages. Despite the poverty or persecution they suffered, people found it difficult to leave their familiar surroundings and brave a wilderness of water, then a wilderness of land.

But as the tales about America continued to spread, more and more settlers came, sometimes singly, sometimes in small groups. Their coming encouraged others to follow. Stouter vessels were built, more suitable for long and stormy voyages. Free land was offered to those who would settle in the New World. Ever larger numbers left the Old World for the fresh and unexplored wilderness of the New World. And as they came, the New World grew.

The first permanent English colony on North American soil was founded in 1607, on a large tract of land named Virginia. The settlers, who came to Virginia to dig for gold and grow rich, soon learned that there was no gold, but that they could grow rich by planting tobacco and sending it to the Old World.

54

In 1620, thirteen years after the founding of Virginia, the Pilgrims set out for this southern colony, where they had been given permission to settle. But they were blown from their course and landed at Cape Cod, where they suffered through a long, bleak winter. Their numbers grew as more Puritans came and settled among them, as well as in Connecticut and along Massachusetts Bay.

All along the seacoast, little English colonies sprang up, plantation colonies in the warm south and farmland towns and villages in the central and northern sections, where the land and climate were not suitable for the cultivation of tobacco, cotton and sugar. Here and there, where coastline and water met to form a natural harbor, wharves were built, ships came to dock, and the settlements, in time, became important harbor cities.

Most of the early Jewish settlers in North America sought the harbor cities, for conditions in the Old World had forced them to be merchants or traders. They had not been permitted to own land, so they knew little about farming. They had not been permitted to practice the crafts, even in friendly Holland, because the craft guilds would not admit them to their ranks. Having been a wandering people, seeking better or safer homes now in one land and now in another, they had friends and relatives throughout Europe, South America, and in the West Indies. They could therefore send cargoes of goods to their friends in other lands and have their friends or agents sell the goods and send back products needed by the colonists in the New World.

Where Jews Did Not Settle

The Puritans had in many ways been influenced by the Jews. They had borrowed ideas from the Hebrew Scriptures. They liked to compare themselves with the early Israelites escaping from Egypt and facing the dangers of the wilderness. They regarded the ancient Jewish government under the rule of the Judges as the ideal form of government. Many of their laws were based on the laws of Moses, and they used Jewish biblical names for their children. When they celebrated their Thanksgiving festival, it was modelled after the Jewish harvest festival, *Sukkot*. When they founded their colleges, Harvard and Yale, the Hebrew language was part of their curriculum.

Yet Jews, except for a single Jew here and there, did not come to the New England Puritan towns. For though the Puritans had come to the New World seeking freedom, they were not ready to give that freedom to others. Governed by their stern church elders, persecuting members of other religious sects who drifted into their colonies, the Puritans did not attract settlers who did not believe as they did.

Nor did many Jews go to Maryland, whose Toleration Act granted freedom of worship to Christians only, nor to Virginia, where the Church of England was the established church. The Jews sought those places in the New World where they could have freedom to live and worship as Jews, and freedom to earn a living.

The Founding of Newport

There lived, in the town of Salem, in Massachusetts, a fiery pastor called Roger Williams, who believed in freedom of worship for all. The church elders of Salem did not approve of Roger Williams, for he was creating a storm in the little town. "I desire not that liberty for myself," he said, "which I would not freely and impartially weigh out to the consciences of the world besides." When Roger Williams refused to be silenced, denouncing the persecution of other religious sects by the Puritans, the elders decided to send him back to England. But Roger Williams was warned in time, and fleeing from Salem, he made his way to an Indian friend. The following spring, in 1636, he bought some land from the Narragansett Indians and founded a colony which he called Providence. This was

the first colony in North America which offered complete religious freedom to all its inhabitants.

It was not long before many victims of discrimination came to live in Providence. In time, other settlements went up near Providence. Of these settlements the most important was Newport, looking out on the Atlantic Ocean and on Narragansett Bay.

Settling in Newport

Jews soon found their way to the seaport town of Newport, a few from New Amsterdam, a few from the West Indies. As Newport slowly developed, more Jewish settlers came, from Holland, from Poland, some Marranos from Spain and Portugal.

In 1752, a young Marrano named Duarte Lopez fled from Portugal and came to Newport with his wife and children, joining his half-brother, Moses, who had been living in the city for some time. As soon as Duarte Lopez and his wife arrived, they followed the custom practiced by many Marranos who came to America. They were re-married, this time according to the Jewish law. Then Duarte took the name of Aaron, and his wife and children also changed their names to Hebrew ones.

Three years later, in 1755, an earthquake shook Lisbon, and thousands of people fled from the city. A group of Marranos from Lisbon set sail for Virginia, but a storm drove their vessel into the harbor of Newport, and here their journey ended. They liked the friendly town looking out upon the sea, and they liked the part their people were playing in the growth of Newport. Some of the earliest settlers followed humble occupations. They were soap-makers, silversmiths, brass workers, candle-makers. Some had become prosperous merchants. Aaron Lopez, who was only twenty-five years old, already had ships sailing to foreign lands, and bringing goods from one settlement to another along the seacoast. The refugees decided to remain in Newport, where they could take part in the life of the growing town.

The Industry of Newport

In the following years the town of Newport grew into a busy, prosperous city. With its growth and prosperity came the growth and prosperity of the Jewish community. Newport's position facing the sea encouraged trading, and vessels owned by Jewish merchants carried goods from one coastal city to another, and went to foreign shores to exchange America's furs, indigo, dried fish, sugar, flax, rice, for the products of the Old World. The imported goods were brought by vessel to the coastal cities, and by pack train to the inland settlements, where pioneers were pushing back the frontier.

Aaron Lopez owned or had a share in thirty vessels. He and other merchants brought more than just the necessities of life to the American colonies. Sometimes there were luxuries, which only the rich could buy. Benjamin Gomez, a Jewish merchant who lived in New York, listed some of the things he had for sale in a letter he wrote to Aaron Lopez: scarlet cloth, crepes, silk, satin, calico, raven duck, Russia sheeting, damasks, printed cotton, fine Irish linen. Other merchants advertised other products they had received from the Old World: Florence oil, Holland velvet, ivory combs, mantuas, India spices, Harlem stripes, true lovers' knots. . . . Hayman Levy, of New York, ran an advertisement to describe his merchandise: Hair Cockades, Castile and Philadelphia Soap, Loaf Sugar, Superfine Hyson Tea, Raisins per the Cask, Cheshire Cheese, Burdeaux Claret, in Hogsheads and Bottles . . . A large and very neat assortment of European and India Goods, Beaver and Deer Leather.

There was also a good deal of slave trade in colonial America. The Jewish merchants of Newport, like other American merchants, sent their ships to the West Indies for molasses, which was brought to the distilleries of Newport. Here the molasses was converted into rum, which was then sent to Africa to be exchanged for slaves.

Women made their own candles in colonial days. This was a long, laborious process, taking months to collect the bits of tallow and hours to melt the tallow and harden it on wicks. Some of the Jewish refugees from Portugal had learned in Lisbon the skill of making candles out of the sperm of whales. Sperm candles were far superior to candles made of tallow, for they gave a stronger, brighter light. When the refugees came to Newport, they made the city the center for the manufacture of sperm candles.

By 1760, the candle-makers of Newport had seventeen factories turning out not only sperm candles, but also sperm oil for lamps. Newport's oil and candles went to foreign and domestic markets. The English house-owner, hanging his sperm candles out at night to light the dark street for the peace and safety of the city, probably did not dream that his candles had come to him from the factories of Aaron and Moses Lopez, or of Jacob Rivera, or Naphtali Hart, pioneer candle-makers of Newport.

Worshipping in Freedom

It was a cold day in December, in the year 1763. A wind blew in from the sea, whispering along the quiet streets. The Jews of Newport, dressed in their finest clothes, in their imported silks and damasks and velvets, the wigs of the men carefully powdered, the jewels of the women catching the late afternoon light, made their way through the cold city to their new synagogue. Dr. Ezra Stiles, the preacher who was to become the first president of Yale University, put on his warmest cloak and went too. For Dr. Stiles was interested in the Jews, the people who stemmed from ancestors who had given the world the Bible. Dr. Stiles was eager to see how services were conducted in a synagogue, for he had never seen a synagogue.

It had taken them a long time to build their synagogue, but they had built it well, asking the finest architect in the New World to design their house of worship. Four years back, in 1759, they had broken ground and six of their most prominent men had each laid a cornerstone. They had needed six cornerstones, four for the synagogue and two for the school attached to it. They had been advised not to attach a school to the building. It would spoil the simple beauty of the architecture, they were told. But they had insisted on building a school. The education of their children, they said, was more important than beauty of architecture.

The money for the building had come in slowly, for though there were wealthy men among them, they were a small community, and some were humble workmen, bakers, snuff-makers, butchers, metal workers. The bricks they had ordered from Europe had arrived the year after the cornerstones had been laid, and had been paid for at once. But there had been many other things to pay for—labor, lumber, glass for the windows, paint, furnishings. They had appealed to the Jews of Jamaica, England, Surinam, to help them. They had all responded, sending gifts for their synagogue, Yeshuat Israel, Salvation of Israel. From the Jews of Amsterdam had come a handsome Torah Scroll, two hundred years old.

But the Jews of New York had helped most. The community that had started with twenty-three refugees from Brazil had already built a small synagogue on Mill Street, the first synagogue in North America. Several times had Shearith Israel, Remnant of Israel, of New York, sent help to Yeshuat Israel of Newport, for it was the habit of Jewish communities to help one another.

The members of Shearith Israel had also sought help in building their synagogue. For a while they had worshipped in an old grist mill, which had once served the Dutch as their church. Then they rented a house owned by a Dutch shoemaker. Finally, about one hundred feet from the wooden building of the shoemaker, they had bought a plot of land to build a synagogue which would also serve

as a school for their children. Help had come to them from many
places. The Chief Rabbi of Curaçao had collected two-hundred and
sixty-four Spanish coins, pieces of eight, and had sent them to
Shearith Israel. Gifts had come from Jamaica, Barbados, London.
Members of the community had paid for single bricks, for bricks,
made by hand and imported from Europe, were very costly in those
days. They contributed the lime, the wax for candles, the windows,
even parts of windows. One man paid for the engraving of the Ten
Commandments, a shilling for each commandment, ten shillings in
all. Finally, on the seventh day of Passover in the year 1730, their
synagogue was ready for dedication. Dressed in their most beautiful clothes, their servants walking behind them carrying their prayer
shawls and their prayerbooks, they went to their little brick synagogue on Mill Street, the street named for the old grist mill where
both the Dutch and they had once worshipped. The synagogue had
been set back from the street in a yard, following the European
custom of building synagogues back from the street, a safeguard,
however slight, against attack. They had passed through the picket
fence on the seventh day of their Festival of Freedom to dedicate
the first synagogue built in the land of freedom.

And now in Newport some thirty years later, another synagogue, Yeshuat Israel, the second in North America, was to be dedicated. This time the dedication was to be on Ḥanukah, on the first day of the Festival of Lights. The descendants of the Maccabees went in triumph to the dedication, as their ancestors had gone before them to dedicate the Temple in Jerusalem. They had built their synagogue in freedom, but because many of them had been Marranos, accustomed to praying in secret, their synagogue had a secret stairway leading from the *bimah* (reader's table) to the basement. Their rabbi, Isaac Touro, who had come to them from Jamaica, awaited their coming. And as the doors were opened his voice rang out in greeting: "Open for me the gates of righteousness!"

"How Came They Here?"

Years went by. The harbor city became one of the most important on the eastern seaboard. The Jewish community flourished, building its own life, contributing to the growth of the city. In the meantime, the young New World was growing restless under the restrictions placed upon her by Britain. At last came the war for independence. British troops invaded Newport. Many Jews, like Aaron Lopez, fled to other cities rather than pledge allegiance to England. Eight thousand British troops entered Newport, and because the people had burned a British ship which had come to exact a tax which the colonists felt was unjust, the soldiers destroyed much of the beautiful city. Never again did the Jewish community of Newport regain the glory of pre-revolutionary days.

But its memory lingered on in the old synagogue on the tree-lined street, on the tombstones of the old cemetery. In August, 1947, the Newport synagogue was dedicated as a national American shrine, while the cemetery, years before the dedication, was immortalized by a poet who came to visit Newport. The poet walked through the shaded cemetery and read the names on the tomb-

stones—Lopez, Pollak, Seixas, Rivera, Touro, Eliezer, Lucena. . . .
In his mind, he saw them, in their glory, in their pride, in their
sorrows. And the poet, Henry Wadsworth Longfellow, wrote a
poem:

> *How strange it seems! These Hebrews in their graves*
> *Close by the street of this fair seaport town,*
> *Silent beside the never-silent waves,*
> *At rest in all this moving up and down!*

> *And these sepulchral stones, so old and brown,*
> *That pave with level flags their burial-place,*
> *Seem like the tablets of the Law, thrown down*
> *And broken by Moses at the mountain's base.*

> *The very names recorded here are strange,*
> *Of foreign accent, and of different climes;*
> *Alvares and Rivera interchange*
> *With Abraham and Jacob of old times.*

> *How came they here? What burst of Christian hate,*
> *What persecution, merciless and blind,*
> *Drove o'er the sea—that desert desolate—*
> *These Ishmaels and Hagars of mankind?*

> *Pride and humiliation hand in hand*
> *Walked with them through the world where'er they went,*
> *Trampled and beaten were they as the sand,*
> *And yet unshaken as the continent.*

Things to Read

Blandford, Benjamin W., *Off the Capes of Delaware,* "In the Days of Witchcraft," pp. 20-32; "David, the Peddler," pp. 78-99; "The Mysterious Mr. Jacobs," pp. 47-61.

Leonard, Oscar, *Americans All,* "The Merchant Prince," pp. 29-34.

Levinger, Elma Ehrlich, *The Golden Door,* "A Place of Refuge," pp. 36-40.

Spitz, Leon, *What the Liberty Bell Proclaimed,* "The Merchant Prince," pp. 29-34.

Questions to Discuss

Discuss Longfellow's poem on the cemetery of Newport. What, in your opinion, prompted him to write the poem? What effect do you think it had on his readers, on their ideas about the Jews?

Make clay models of the Mill Street and the Newport synagogues.

Teachers Bibliography

Freund, Miriam, *Jewish Merchants in Colonial America,* Behrman House, New York, 1939.

Friedman, Lee M., *Pilgrims in a New Land,* Jewish Publication Society, Philadelphia, "The Touro Synagogue of Newport," pp. 119-145.

Gutstein, Morris A., *The Story of the Jews of Newport,* Bloch Publishing Company, New York, 1936.

Learsi, Rufus, *The Jews in America,* pp. 31-32.

Lebeson, Anita, *Pilgrim People,* pp. 57-73.

Marcus, Jacob Rader, *Early American Jewry,* Volume One, pp. 34-197.

CHAPTER 5

Where Liberty Called

In Penn's Domain

It was not an uncommon thing for a king of England to give a tract of land in America to one of his favorites. Or sometimes land was given in payment of a debt, or to a group of people willing to brave the wilderness so that they could live according to their own ideas. William Penn was given the land now called Pennsylvania by King Charles II, who owed a large sum of money to William Penn's father. Since Penn was a Quaker, many Quakers, perse-cuted in England, came to the wilderness on the Delaware which King Charles liked to call Pennsylvania, or "Penn's Woods." It was fertile, virgin land they came to, with hills, valleys, plateaus and rivers, land without towns or farms or highways.

"I know of no religion," said William Penn, "which destroys courtesy, civility and kindness." So the Jews came to Pennsylvania, along with the Mennonites, Baptists, Sabbatarians, Dunkers, Well-Wishers, Presbyterians, Catholics, Lutherans. . . . Philadelphia, the City of Brotherly Love, was laid out by its Quaker founders. Other land was cleared, in time, by new settlers, and more towns were built. Land was cheap in Penn's domain, ten dollars for a hundred acres. A man who might not have been able to afford land in

England or Germany could come to the rich land along the Delaware River and clear the trees and put up a makeshift house till he could afford to build a better one. Sometimes a man bought a large tract of land and sold parcels of it to other settlers. Aaron Levy bought such a tract and laid out the town of Aaronsburg, with a street named for his wife, Rachel's Way, and an intersecting street named for himself, Aaron's Square.

Pioneer Merchants

Jews, coming with the early settlers, helped clear the land and build stockades. Often a Jewish settler put up a rude hut to serve as a trading post where Indians came with their furs. As the population increased, the trading posts grew in size and in number.

There were no good travelling roads in colonial days. The waterways were the best roads between settlements and towns. Flatboats, rafts and canoes carried goods from one place to another. In the lonely settlement on a river's edge, with only the forest behind it, the pioneers waited eagerly for the loaded canoes and flatboats to bring them their sugar and coffee, their fabrics and dried fish and molasses and flour. Merchants bought furs from the Indians, shipped the furs to Newport or New York or Boston, and received in return the supplies needed by the pioneers—sugar, coffee, pots, pans, calico, blankets, boots, dried fish. . . . If a settlement could not be reached by water, the merchant loaded his pack trains, wagons drawn by horses, and sent them down the Indian trails to the pioneer settlements, or blazed new trails through the forests.

Philadelphia, Lancaster, Easton grew. Little stores went up along their main streets. Joseph Simon, a Jewish merchant, opened a general store in Lancaster. Indians came to Joseph Simon's store with their furs, which they exchanged for trinkets, axes, rum, pots, bells, knives, cloth, scissors—goods which Joseph Simon imported from Newport or New York. When Joseph Simon's pack trains left for the settlements beyond the frontier, they carried goods that had come to him from the cities of the Old World and from the coastal cities of the New World. Up and down the rivers and their tributaries Simon sent his goods to the pioneers on the fringe of the wilderness, to men and women depending upon him for the necessities, and a few luxuries, of life.

David Franks too was a Jewish merchant. He lived in Philadelphia, where the trim brick and wooden houses multiplied as time went by. Franks had a counting house on the wharf, which was the busiest part of town, and he owned vessels which he used for coastal and foreign trade.

The Gratz Brothers

One day in 1754, a young man, Barnard Gratz, came to see David Franks. He was a resident of England, the young man told Franks, and he had a brother, Michael, who was on a business trip to India. The brothers were born in Upper Silesia, but they had left their native land because of its many restrictions on the Jews and had gone to England to live. While in England, Barnard had heard many stories about America, and he had come to see what opportunities the land offered.

David Franks gave Barnard a job in his counting house near the busy wharves. The young man learned how to trade with the Indians. He learned about the frontier settlements, and about the western prairies and the valleyland still uninhabited by white man. He saw the many opportunities the New World held for the pioneer, and he wrote to Michael to come to America.

Michael came and took his brother's place in David Franks' counting house, while Barnard set himself up in his own business. And Michael too saw the vision of America—the march of pioneers through the narrow passes and over the mountain ranges, the wagons rolling through green valleys and prairies toward the setting sun, the lonely towns on the riverbanks growing into busy cities. He saw in his mind's eye a continent with cities, towns, villages, farmland, inhabited by people of all races and creeds. And Michael too wanted to become part of America.

Soon Michael and Barnard were in business together, and like the country in which they lived, their horizons opened wider and wider. Their barges and pack trains carried goods to every inhabited part of North America. As the pioneers pushed farther westward, the pack trains of the Gratz brothers followed in their trail. They traded with the merchants of Newport, New York, Georgia, Quebec, London, the West Indies. Their agents sold the Gratz cargoes in England, Holland, Italy, Ireland, Guadaloupe, India, Persia. The Gratz brothers became two of the leading pioneer merchants in colonial America, helping to push her frontier farther and farther westward.

Early Settlers in the Carolinas

South of Virginia, stretching for many miles inland from the coast, lay the rich acres of land called Carolina, granted by Charles II to eight noblemen in 1663. People of many different faiths came to settle here, for John Locke, the English philosopher who drew up the constitution for the colony, had made religious freedom the law of the land. "No person whatsoever," he wrote, "shall disturb, molest or persecute another for his speculative opinions in religion, or his way of worship." And speaking of the Jews, Locke wrote, "If we allow the Jews to have private houses and dwelling places among us, why should we not allow them to have synagogues?"

Political freedom, the right to vote and hold office, was still a rare thing for the Jews, whether in the Old World or in the New World. But since Carolina, like Pennsylvania, New York and Rhode Island, offered them religious and economic freedom, Jews came to Carolina early in its history.

In time, the territory of Carolina was divided, part of it called North Carolina and part of it called South Carolina. In South Carolina large plantations were developed, with slaves to cultivate the crops. In North Carolina there was little slavery. Here the farms were owned by hard working colonists who sowed their own seed and reaped their own harvests.

In neither of the Carolinas did the Jews become farmers. Unaccustomed to tilling the soil, most of the early Jewish settlers were traders. Yet it was a Jewish settler who was responsible for improving the quality of one of South Carolina's most important products.

Moses Lindo

Moses Lindo, a London resident and an expert in indigo, came to South Carolina in 1756 to buy indigo and send it back to English dyers. But so pleased was Lindo with the New World that he decided to remain. As Lindo taught the planters of South Carolina to improve their indigo, more and more land was used to raise the product. Six years after his arrival, Lindo was appointed Surveyor and Inspector-General of Indigo. Thousands of pounds of the product passed through the hands of the Inspector-General before being shipped to Europe. Inspecting cask after cask of the important blue dye, discussing with the planters ways of further improving their valuable product, Lindo contributed to the economic development of South Carolina.

James Oglethorpe's Plan

England was not a happy place for many people in the days of King George I. Thousands of poor men roamed the city streets looking for work. Debtors were imprisoned, and many of them languished in dark, narrow cells for the remainder of their lives.

James Oglethorpe, a member of Parliament, was roused by the condition of the English prisons. Thinking of the unhappy lot of thousands of debtors spending their days under the charge of brutal guards, he came to the king with a plan for transporting large numbers of them to the shores of America. A colony in the southern part of North America would also be to England's benefit, Oglethorpe explained. It would cultivate products needed by England, and serve as a buffer settlement between the English colonies to the north and the Spanish settlement in Florida and the French on the Gulf of Mexico and on the Mississippi River.

The king granted Oglethorpe a large tract of land, and a board of trustees was formed to direct the affairs of the new colony. Committees of men volunteered to raise money to pay for the passage of the colonists and for helping them settle in America. Early in 1733, Oglethorpe set out with the first of the colonists, one hundred and twenty debtors. In February, on a pine covered bluff overlooking the Savannah River, on the territory named Georgia in honor of King George, the settlement of Savannah was founded.

Jewish Pioneers in Savannah

There were several Jews among the men in London who had raised money for the settlers of Georgia. It happened that a number of impoverished Jews, most of them immigrants from the Germanic lands, were living in London at this time. The Jews who had collected funds for the Georgia settlement believed that a good solution to the problem of how to help the German Jews was to send them to America, where they would be able to support themselves. Using some of the money they had collected, they chartered a vessel and sent twelve Jewish families to Georgia.

Oglethorpe and his settlers were celebrating the founding of Savannah when the group of Jews arrived. Most of the English settlers had never seen any Jews, but remembering all the strange tales they had heard about them, disapproved of having them as their neighbors. But Oglethorpe, who did not share the prejudice of his followers, permitted the newcomers to remain.

Several months later another group of Jews came to Georgia from London. These were not German Jews, like those who had come before them. Most of them were Marranos, refugees from Portugal who had found temporary homes in England before sailing for America. Dr. Samuel Nuñez, one of the newcomers, had been a physician at the court of Lisbon. But when he was informed by a friend that he was being followed by spies of the Inquisition who suspected him of practicing the Jewish customs in secret, Dr. Nuñez fled with his family from Portugal to England. From England, he had sailed to Georgia.

The trustees in England did not like what was happening in Georgia. They wanted Georgia to be a Christian colony, and they wrote to Oglethorpe, ordering him to send the Jews away. But Ogle-

thorpe closed his ears to the demands of the trustees. He wrote them
that the Jews were good colonists, industrious and dependable.
Moreover, Oglethorpe informed the trustees, there was a physician
among them, Dr. Samuel Nuñez, who was taking care of the sick in
the colony. The trustees wrote again, repeating their orders, but
again Oglethorpe ignored their prejudices, and the Jews remained.

Jewish Life on the Frontier

Building civilization in a wilderness, and at the same time maintaining their own way of life, was often difficult for the few thousand
Jews in colonial America. Now and then Jewish settlers drifted away
from their religion and customs. But most of them clung to their
own faith, however difficult the conditions around them. Wherever
they went, they wanted to be together, in life and in death. So a small
group of Jewish settlers would buy a bit of land, as soon as they
could, to be used as their burial ground. Building a synagogue was
more costly, and they met in private homes for prayer till they could
put up a real house of worship. Joseph Simon of Lancaster established a synagogue, probably in his own home. When Michael or
Barnard Gratz came to Lancaster from Philadelphia, or if someone
came in from Savannah or New York, he knew where to go for
prayer, to Joseph Simon's home.

In the 1750's the handful of Jews in Philadelphia worshipped in a
rented room on Sterling Street. About ten years later, they decided
it was time to build a synagogue, though they were still very few
in number. They dispatched a messenger to New York to buy a
Sefer Torah. But they found that they had miscalculated. They still
could not afford to build a house of prayer. Several more years went
by, and when they had grown to about a dozen families they tried
again. They got another *Sefer Torah* from Jonas Phillips in New
York, and Barnard Gratz wrote to two of his agents in London for
a silver pointer for the Torah and for some Hebrew prayerbooks.

But the Jews of Philadelphia still had to wait for their synagogue. Though Mikveh Israel, Hope of Israel, was founded in 1740, it was not till the latter days of the Revolution, when many Jewish refugees came to Philadelphia from cities occupied by the British, that the congregation was finally able to build its synagogue.

The Jews of Charleston too took a long time to put up a synagogue. In 1749 they finally had enough Jews to form a congregation, which they called Beth Elohim Unveh Shallom, the House of God and Dwelling of Peace. Some forty years later, the congregation, now numbering about fifty families, received a state charter, this time as Kahal Kadosh Beth Elohim, Congregation of the House of God. The following year, in 1792, they laid the cornerstone of a new synagogue, Beth Elohim, House of God.

When the first group of Jewish pioneers came to Savannah, they brought with them a *Sefer Torah* and immediately established a congregation. Before long they received several gifts, a Ḥanukah menorah and some Hebrew books to strengthen their communal life on the frontier.

Though they were surrounded by people whose customs were different from their own, the Jewish pioneers managed to observe their own Sabbath and festivals. The Gratz brothers did not write on the Sabbath, nor did they do business, however pressing it seemed. An Irish agent of Michael Gratz who had taken a long journey and was waiting for orders, received no word from Philadelphia because it was Shavuot, and Michael Gratz was observing the festival. Because Moses stood on Mount Sinai hundreds of years back, the jocular Irishman complained, Michael Gratz found it necessary to suspend business. When Michael, after a perilous journey in 1784, reached St. Kitts, he wanted to let his brother know that he had arrived safely. But the Sabbath was approaching, so his note was brief. "Being just Sh'b't," he explained the reason for its brevity to his brother. Two Jewish partners in Lancaster, Jacob and Levi, did not want to disappoint their Christian customers, should they come to their store on Saturday and find it closed. So they put a notice in a newspaper announcing that they did not do business on Saturday because they were Jews.

Jews moved about a good deal, in those days, particularly if they were traders. They therefore had the problem of food, especially of *kosher* meat. "I send you," wrote David Hays to his brother Michael in 1784, "by Jacob, ¼ mutton kil'd yesterday. . . . wish you a good . . . . shabos, also Monday is yorsite (*yahrzeit*) for Mother." David wanted to make sure that his brother not only had *kosher* meat, but that, following the Jewish custom, he would light a candle on the anniversary of his mother's death.

Not all the Jews had brothers like David to send them *kosher* meat when they were stranded at some outpost. Records show that in proportion to their numbers, there was an unusually large per-centage of *shoḥtim*, ritual slaughterers, among them. So that if a Jewish traveller found himself in some place where there were no Jews, he could always provide his own *kosher* meat.

Though the Jews of early America were helping to conquer the wilderness, they did not let the wilderness conquer their own way of life.

Things to Read

Blandford, Benjamin W., *Off the Capes of Delaware,* "A Jew Among Quakers," pp. 101-116; "From Debtor's Prison," pp. 117-126; "The Yellow Topaz," pp. 155-167.

Levinger, Elma Ehrlich, *The Golden Door,* "The Little Jew of Lancas-ter," pp. 65-93.

Questions to Discuss

Discuss William Penn's statement, "I know of no religion which destroys courtesy, civility and kindness."

Why was it difficult for prejudice against the Jews to continue to flourish, as it had in the Old World, in a frontier settlement like Savannah?

Things to Do

Write to Brandon Films, Inc., 200 West 57th Street, New York 19, N. Y., for the film, "The Aaronsburg Story."

Pretend you are Dr. Samuel Nuñez. Write his diary, beginning with his flight from Portugal.

Teachers Bibliography

Goodman, Abram Vassen, *American Overture,* Jewish Publication Society, Philadelphia, 1947.

Handlin, Oscar, *Adventure in Freedom,* McGraw-Hill Book Company, New York, 1954, pp. 3-21.

Learsi, Rufus, *The Jews in America,* pp. 32-38.

Lebeson, Anita, *Pilgrim People,* pp. 74-118.

UNIT TWO BUILDING
FREEDOM

CHAPTER 1

Rebellion Against Tyrants

The Colonial Spirit

When England emerged victorious from the Seven Years War in Europe and, in 1763, from the French and Indian War in America, she found herself heavily in debt. To help rid herself of her debt, England decided to increase taxation of the American colonies. Parliament, whose members were usually rich landowners, realized that the New World could serve England as a source of revenue. By taxing the colonists, by using America's raw materials to make English goods, and by using America as a market for these goods, England could strengthen her financial and economic position.

But in planning to use the American colonies for enriching and strengthening herself, England did not reckon with the spirit of the colonists. The French and Indian War had given them a feeling of self-reliance they had never had before. Since the earliest days of colonization, this feeling had been steadily growing. The refugee from oppression, the bond servant whose passage to America had been paid for by a master whom he was obliged to serve in the New World for a number of years, the unemployed craftsman seized in the streets of London and sent to America, all had learned to know independence. They had hacked away forests, crossed mountains, built cities. They had learned how to manufacture their own goods and sail the seas in search of markets. They had developed their local governments as well as leaders to speak for them and lead them. They were prepared to resist oppression, even if it meant war.

Resistance to taxation without representation in Parliament grew stronger among the colonists. Blindly, Britain tried force to bend the colonists to her will. Finally came the shot heard round the world. It was in April, 1775, that General Gage's troops fired on a group of minutemen who had gathered at Lexington. America rose in defense of the freedom she had built.

The Hebrew Bible

As the Jews had contributed to the growth of America, so they contributed to America's love of freedom. Their Bible, with its emphasis on freedom and justice, had been the Book of Books of the early colonists. It had a prominent place in every Puritan home. The farmer, resting from his labors, reached for the family Bible. Over and over again he read the old familiar story of the Israelites leaving the slavery of Egypt for the freedom of the Promised Land, or the story of Samuel warning his people that choosing a king to rule them meant losing their freedom. The preacher, looking for a text for his sermon, turned to his well-thumbed Bible, deliberating on whether to choose a verse from the prophet Amos or a verse from the prophet Isaiah.

England, to the early Puritans, was Egypt, where they had been oppressed by a Pharaoh, King James I. The Atlantic Ocean was the Red Sea, America was Canaan, the Promised Land, and Boston was Jerusalem. When the Pilgrims wanted names for their children they went to the Bible. They based many of their laws on those of the Jews. And following the custom of the Jews, they made the

Sabbath a day of rest and began it on the evening of the preceding day. There was also other Sabbatarians who modelled their Sabbath after that of the Jews, changing Sunday from the Lord's Day to a Sabbath, a day of rest. The New England Primer, which was the textbook of the Puritan primary schools for five generations, consisted of little verses, each beginning with a letter of the alphabet, and each verse based on a biblical character: Job feels the rod, yet blesses God; Samuel anoints, and God appoints. . . .

Hebrew in Colonial America

Because the Bible was important in colonial America, Hebrew too was important. Protestant ministers were expected to know Hebrew so that they could read the Bible in its original language. When Harvard, the first college established in America, opened in 1638 as a school for training Protestant ministers, Hebrew was one of the required subjects. Ezra Stiles, president of Yale, learned his Hebrew from Jews. Samuel Johnson, first president of King's College, now Columbia, required all his tutors to know Hebrew. The first Hebrew book printed in America was a Hebrew grammar which was meant to be used by college students. Yale chose for the words on its seal the Hebrew words *Urim V'Tumim*, the words that had been engraved on the breastplates of the priests in the Temple of Jerusalem, while the seal of King's College, which later changed its name to Columbia University, had the Hebrew name of God.

In some colleges, the students were expected to write their graduation theses in Hebrew. Often a college student turned in a thesis on the Hebrew language. "Hebrew Is the Mother of Languages," was the subject chosen by one student. And another: "By contracting sentences the Hebrews expand the meaning." There was a widespread belief in those days that the Indians were descendants of the Ten Lost Tribes. One student at Harvard chose as his subject, "Are the Americans Israelites?" Many chose subjects based on the Bible: "Was the destruction of the world by Noah's deluge brought about by natural causes?" Or, "Have the original texts of the Bible come down to us pure and uncorrupted?"

Ideas as Weapons

In a land where the Bible was so important, it was no wonder that its ideals influenced the thinking of many people. The Americans, declared Dr. Ezra Stiles, were God's American Israel, and George Washington was Joshua, leading his people to freedom. The prophet Samuel had warned the Israelites against having a king, a Boston preacher reminded his congregation. Should not the Americans too heed the warning and rid themselves of the king of England? Nor did it seem strange to a people familiar with the Bible to have inscribed on the Liberty Bell words taken from the Bible: "Proclaim liberty throughout the land, unto all the inhabitants thereof" (Leviticus, 25:10).

The Founding Fathers of the Republic were students of the Bible, familiar with the history of the Jews and their ideals of freedom and justice. When Benjamin Franklin, John Adams and Thomas Jefferson were asked to design a seal for the new government, the subject they thought most fitting was a picture of the Israelites pursued by Pharaoh as they crossed the Red Sea, and around the picture the words: "Rebellion Against Tyrants Is Obedience to God."

"Hebraic mortar," it was said, "cemented the foundations of American democracy." The old Jewish ideals, enduring through the ages, became a heritage of the American people.

Things to Read

Read Samuel's advice to the Children of Israel about choosing a king. You will find it in First Samuel, chapter 8, verses 10-19.

Questions to Discuss

Discuss the influence of the Bible on the American ideals of freedom.
What subjects taken from the Bible other than the one chosen by Jefferson, Adams and Franklin would you consider appropriate for a seal for the new American government?
Discuss Samuel's advice to the Children of Israel concerning a king.

Things to Do

Leaf through the pages of the prophets Amos and Hosea to see if you can find some mottoes for the Liberty Bell.

Teachers Bibliography

Friedman, Lee M., *Pilgrims in a New Land,* "Biblia Americana," pp. 15-30.
Learsi, Rufus, *The Jews in America,* pp. 32-38.
Lebeson, Anita, *Pilgrim People,* pp. 39-53.

CHAPTER **2**

Heroes of the Revolution

Taking Sides

There were about two thousand Jews in the colonies when the struggle with England began, only a small fraction of the general population. But their contribution to the revolution far outweighed their small numbers. Not all the colonists were patriots. Some preferred to remain loyal to England, the mother country. There were Tories, or loyalists, among the Jews, just as there were among other sections of the population. But the vast majority threw in their lot with the young government seeking to free herself from the domination of the Old World.

Jewish merchants, like the Gratz brothers, signed the Non-Importation Resolutions, pledging to buy no English goods till the Stamp Act was repealed. With the permission of the government, Jewish merchants equipped their vessels with cannon and sent them out to prey on British ships. Together with other revolutionary privateers, they helped capture about seven hundred British vessels, inflicting a loss of about eighteen million dollars to British merchants. In whatever way they could, the Jews served their country in its war for independence.

86

Francis Salvador

In the year 1773 a young man, Francis Salvador, left his home in London and set sail for Charleston, South Carolina. It had not been an easy matter for the young man to leave his wife and four children and the luxuries he had always enjoyed in England for the harsher life of America. His ancestors had been wealthy Portuguese Marranos. Some of them had migrated to Holland, then to England. Francis Salvador had married the daughter of his uncle, Joseph Salvador, one of the richest men in London. Joseph Salvador had investments in the Dutch East India Company as well as in Lisbon. He had bought seven thousand acres of land in faraway South Carolina, though he did not intend to live there. Suddenly came the earthquake in Lisbon and the failure of the Dutch East India Company, and the Salvadors found that their fortunes had dwindled. It was then that Francis Salvador thought of the acres of uncultivated land in South Carolina. He decided he would recoup the family fortunes by putting the land under cultivation. And after preparing a suitable home for them, he would send for his wife and children.

Francis Salvador built his plantation home at Coronaca Creek. Soon many acres of land were planted with indigo, and Salvador bought slaves to tend his fields and manor. The young Jewish aristocrat from London made friends with other plantation owners, and it was not long before he was drawn into the political ferment of the day. Some of Salvador's neighbors believed it was time for the colonies to free themselves of the mother country. Others believed just as strongly in remaining subject to England. Coming from a rich, aristocratic family, Salvador might have been expected to join with the Tories, as many wealthy men and women did. Instead, he found himself sympathizing with the rebels and working with them.

Francis Salvador threw himself into his revolutionary work with such ardor that he was sent to the South Carolina Provincial Con-

gress in Charleston as one of the deputies of his district. There, with
Pinckney and other revolutionary leaders, he worked for America's
independence.

Across the border of South Carolina lived the Cherokee Indians.
When the struggle with England began, the English made friends
with the Indians, promising them land and money if they won the
war against the colonists.

Late in June, in the summer of 1776, a British fleet sailed into
the harbor of Charleston to attack the colony. Several days later, on
July 1, the Cherokee Indians invaded from the rear, crossing the
frontier of South Carolina. The fighting spread, and Major Andrew
Williamson, like Salvador a member of the Provincial Congress, was
appointed to command the militia of the outlying regions.

One morning in July a young man came stumbling into Salvador's
house, his hand bleeding where two fingers had been shot off. Briefly
he told Salvador what had happened. The Cherokees had attacked

his home, killing his father, Captain Smith, his mother, and two of his brothers and sisters. He alone had managed to escape.

Francis Salvador quickly mounted his horse and galloped off in the direction of Major Williamson's house, twenty-eight miles away. He passed farmers in flight, cornfields and houses burning, panic-stricken women and children running along the roads. At last he drew up his horse before the Major's house and rushed in with the news of the Indian attack.

The Major sent out messengers in every direction to round up the militiamen, but hundreds of them had fled, so great was their fear of the Indians and of the Tories, disguised as Indians, who fought with them. When Major Williamson and Francis Salvador set out for the late Captain Smith's house, they had only forty men with them. As they rode along, however, others joined them, so that they finally had five hundred men to throw back the Cherokees.

On August 1, as the detachment was passing through the village of Essenecca, shots suddenly rang out from behind trees and fences. Too late they discovered that they had walked into an ambush. The Major's horse was shot away from under him. Francis Salvador received three shots and fell from his horse into the bushes, where he was pounced upon by the Indians and scalped.

An hour later the battle was over. The Indians had fled. Major Williamson knelt beside his dying friend. At the sound of the Major's voice Salvador opened his eyes and asked whether the enemy had been defeated. Hearing that the battle had been won, Salvador took the Major's hand, told him he was satisfied, and closing his eyes, breathed his last, the first Jew to give his life in the war for freedom. On his tombstone were engraved the words:

Born an aristocrat, he became a democrat,
An Englishman, he cast his lot with America;
True to his ancient faith, he gave his life
For new hopes of human liberty and understanding.

The Very Great Rebel

Mordecai Sheftall, of Georgia, had good reason to be proud of himself, for the British called him a "very great rebel."

Mordecai Sheftall had lived in Georgia all his life. His father, Benjamin, whose native land was Germany, had migrated to England, and from there he had come to Savannah on the boat which had brought the group of Spanish-Portuguese Jews. Two years later Mordecai was born. The boy learned many things from his father and neighbors, how to plant and reap, how to handle cows and horses. He liked to spend his idle hours at the wharves and near the river, where many merchants had their warehouses. By the time Mordecai reached manhood he owned hundreds of acres of land, a sawmill, and a large warehouse near the river.

Mordecai Sheftall became a prominent man in Savannah as well as a leader in his own small community. By 1774 there were no more than ten Jewish families in the city, still not enough to build a synagogue. Sheftall furnished a room in his house to serve as a synagogue and invited his people to worship there. He also gave the small congregation several acres of land to be used as a cemetery and as a site for a synagogue.

There were many Tories in Georgia, particularly among the wealthier people. But Mordecai Sheftall did not hesitate to join the rebel side. When Sheftall was made chairman of a rebel committee, called the Parochial Committee, he would stand at the wharf, where British ships came to unload, and order the captain to leave with his ship and cargo. The Governor of Georgia, who was appointed by Britain, wrote letters to the government in England complaining about the Parochial Committee and particularly about its chairman who dared issue orders to British captains to leave the king's port. Often the Tories of Georgia struck back at Sheftall, and once his ranch was raided and some of his slaves were carried off to Florida.

When Sheftall was appointed to the staff of the Georgia Brigade, his task was to supply food and arms for the militia of Georgia. The following year he was given another assignment, to supply food and clothes to the Continental troops of South Carolina and Georgia.

Before the last appointment could be approved by Congress, Sheftall, his son, and a number of officers and privates were captured by the British during a surprise attack. Sheftall was brought before the British commissary officer for questioning. When Sheftall stubbornly refused to reveal where the American supplies were kept, he was removed with his son and other prisoners to a prison ship. He remained on the ship for several months, suffering hunger and abuse. At last he was exchanged for a British prisoner of war, and a short time later, his son was also released. Ever after, Mordecai Sheftall proudly referred to himself as a "very great rebel."

The Patriot Leader

In August, 1776, Lord Howe's fleet appeared in the harbor of New York City. George Washington, who had been defeated at Long Island and had withdrawn to New York, decided that he must continue the retreat, for his troops were not ready to make a stand. For the time being, he must leave New York in the hands of the British.

In the historic little synagogue of Shearith Israel, the leader of the congregation, the *ḥazan*, Gershom Mendes Seixas (pronounced Say-shus), with a group of followers, gathered together the holy objects, the Torah Scrolls, the prayerbooks, the candlesticks. Gershom Seixas knew that he must flee from New York, for to remain meant to pledge allegiance to Britain, and this he would not do. Not all the members of his congregation were patriots. Some of the rich members, satisfied with their lives of ease and luxury, did not know what changes the revolution would bring, and they preferred to have things remain as they were. But the majority sided with their *ḥazan,* who had made many stirring sermons for the patriot cause.

As Gershom Seixas was stripping his synagogue, other members of the congregation were also preparing to leave the city before Lord Howe took over. Jonas Phillips, a merchant, felt that freedom was more important than the business he had built up. So he took his wife and fifteen children and left New York for Philadelphia, where he enlisted in the militia as a private.

Isaac Moses, a rich merchant, also left his home in New York and went to Philadelphia, where he served in the militia. Being a wealthy man who owned numerous vessels, he outfitted many of them with cannon, and like Robert Morris, Aaron Lopez, and other revolutionary privateers, sent them out to prey on English ships.

Hayman Levy was another merchant to flee from New York. Leaving his home and his large stock of merchandise, he went to Philadelphia and joined the militia, although he was already in his late sixties.

Gershom Seixas, accompanied by his family and by some members of his congregation, fled from New York five days before Washington evacuated the city. The group went first to Stratford, Connecticut, where they lived for four years. Then, taking with them the holy objects they had brought from their synagogue in New York, they went on to Philadelphia, the seat of the American government.

The Jews of Philadelphia were happy to welcome Gershom Seixas and his friends. For a long time the congregation, Mikveh Israel, had wanted a synagogue. Up to the time of the revolution, they had worshipped in private homes, then in rented rooms. The revolution had brought Jewish refugees from cities the British had captured, and now, with the arrival of Seixas, a campaign was begun to collect money for building a synagogue.

Money was raised, land was bought, and builders were hired. With Gershom Seixas as its spiritual leader, the synagogue was dedicated in 1782. Hayman Levy of New York, who had contributed eighty pounds for building the synagogue, was given the honor of opening the doors of the Ark. Gershom Seixas remained in Philadelphia till the war was over, then, recalled by Shearith Israel, he returned to New York, bringing back the holy objects he had taken with him for safekeeping.

Haym Salomon

Not long before the outbreak of the revolution, a young Polish Jew, Haym Salomon, arrived in New York. Coming from Poland, a land where his people were oppressed, Haym Salomon joined a patriot organization called the Sons of Liberty. When the British entered New York, Salomon was seized as a spy and held in Provost prison.

A Hessian general soon discovered that the Jewish immigrant from Poland was too valuable a man to be kept locked up. Salomon had travelled through Europe before coming to America, and besides Polish, he was able to speak German, French, Italian, English and Russian. There were many men in Provost prison with whom the Hessian general found it difficult to communicate. There were Frenchmen, for example, who had come to America to help her fight for her independence. The Hessian general decided that he would use Salomon as his interpreter, and so gave him his freedom.

During the brief period of liberty he enjoyed, Haym Salomon married Rachel Franks. But the young bride was soon deprived of her husband. It was rumored that Salomon, moving freely among the prisoners, had helped some of the Frenchmen and Americans escape. Putting his knowledge of German to good use, he had also persuaded some of the Hessian soldiers to desert. The Hessian soldiers had been hired out by the ruler of Hesse to fight for King George, and they had no real interest in the war. If they deserted to the American lines, Salomon told them, they would receive free land.

Again coming under suspicion, Haym Salomon was forced to flee from New York. Leaving his wife and child till he could send for them, he went to Philadelphia, where he arrived almost penniless. He was heard from again several years later, when he opened a small broker's office on Front Street. In a short time Haym Salomon re-established himself. Hundreds of thousands of dollars passed through his hands, for he had a rare gift for finances. This gift he put at the disposal of the government.

Salomon became the treasurer of the French troops in America, selling their bills of exchange. Robert Morris, Superintendent of Finance of the American government, used Salomon as one of his agents for raising money to supply the troops and to run the government. As the war dragged on, the needs of the government increased, and Morris turned more and more to Salomon. The soldiers were badly equipped, some without uniforms, some without boots or shoes. There was a shortage of food, of blankets, of ammunition. The broker on Front Street was kept busy day and night raising money, often advancing his own to the government. Representatives in Congress often received no salary, for the government had no money to give them. But they knew that Salomon would help them. James Madison wrote to a friend, "The kindness of our little friend in Front Street near the coffee-house, is a fund that will preserve me from extremities, but I never resort to it without mortification, as he obstinately rejects all recompense. . . . To a necessitous delegate, he gratuitously spares a supply out of his private stock."

Weakened by his imprisonment and by his work in Philadelphia, Haym Salomon died when he was forty-five years old, all his fortune gone. In the city of Chicago, in 1941, a monument was erected to the memory of the little broker on Front Street. The monument has

three figures. In the center stands George Washington, clasping, on his left, the hand of Robert Morris, and on his right, the hand of Haym Salomon, the man who had given all he had for liberty.

Heroes in the Ranks

Jews fought on every battlefield, as privates and as officers.

David Minis fought in Georgia, then in South Carolina.

David Cardoza, of Charleston, served in Captain Lushington's Company, like other Jews of the city.

Joseph Solomon, also of Charleston, died in battle.

Phillip Moses Russell served as surgeon's mate in Virginia.

Solomon Simson, of New York, served in the New York militia. He also supplied cannon to New York colonial troops, and lead for making bullets.

Benjamin Nones came from France in 1777 and immediately enlisted. Cited for gallant action, Nones became a Major and commanded a company of four hundred men, of whom many were Jews.

Captain Jacob Cohen served under Lafayette.

Michael Moses Hart, Reuben Etting, Jacob Leon, Abraham Seixas, Nathaniel Levy, Isaac Israel, Aaron Benjamin, David Hays ... The list goes on and on, though the names of many have been forgotten. As happens in all wars, many died unsung on the field of battle.

Things to Read

Alofsin, Dorothy, *America's Triumph,* U.A.H.C., Cincinnati, 1949, "For Love of Liberty," pp. 15-36.

Blandford, Benjamin W., *Off the Capes of Delaware,* "In the Days of the Regulators," pp. 190-203; "They Made a Covenant," pp. 218-232.

Fast, Howard, *Haym Salomon, Son of Liberty,* Julian Messner, Inc., New York, 1941.

Leonard, Oscar, *Americans All,* "And Some Helped Washington," pp. 35-46; "The Jewish Paul Revere," pp. 47-58; "He Hated Slavery," pp. 59-63; "He Scored a Point," pp. 74-78.

Levinger, Elma Ehrlich, *The Golden Door,* "The Generous Giver," pp. 94-109; "The Last Service," pp. 52-64.

Lurie, Rose G., *The Great March,* "For Liberty," pp. 116-130.

Pessin, Deborah, *Giants on the Earth,* "Son of Liberty," pp. 76-88.

Spitz, Leon, *What the Liberty Bell Proclaimed,* "What the Liberty Bell Proclaimed," pp. 67-76.

Questions to Discuss

What do the last two lines on Salvador's tombstone mean?

Discuss the statement, "Hebraic mortar cemented the foundations of American democracy."

Things to Do

Write to the Jewish Education Film Library, 13 East 37th St., New York 16, N. Y., for the film, "Sons of Liberty." You may also want to see the filmstrip, "The Story of Haym Salomon," which is distributed by American Jewish Archives, Clifton Avenue, Cincinnati 20, Ohio.

Teachers Bibliography

Friedman, Lee M., *Jewish Pioneers and Patriots,* "George Washington and the Jews of His Day," pp. 13-30.

Friedman, Lee M., *Pilgrims in a New Land,* "Haym Salomon—Freedom's Financier," pp. 58-70; "A Messenger to General Washington," pp. 71-78.

Handlin, Oscar, *Adventure in Freedom,* pp. 22-37.

CHAPTER **3**

Religious Freedom

Peace

Peace came at last. The men returned to their homes, to the farms and shops they had left to take up arms in defense of their way of life. A grateful people chose George Washington President of their Republic. Many letters of congratulations and good wishes came to the first President from the people of the country. Among these were letters from the six Jewish congregations, one from Savannah, one from Newport, and one, a joint letter, from the congregations of Charleston, Philadelphia, New York, and the new congregation of Richmond, Beth Shalom, House of Peace.

Washington responded to the letters he received. In his letter to the Newport congregation, Washington expressed an idea which was very new to the world. At a time when tolerance of other people's religious beliefs and way of life was something which few people accepted, Washington, like other founders of the Republic, had already reached the point in his thinking where mere tolerance was not enough. For tolerance implied that a person had the right to tolerate or not to tolerate another man's personal beliefs. Washington believed that all men were entitled to believe and worship as they wished, and that no man had the right to deprive another man of his rights because his way of life was different.

"The citizens of the United States," wrote Washington in his letter to Newport, "have a right to applaud themselves for having given to mankind examples of an enlarged and liberal policy worthy of imitation. All possess alike liberty of conscience and immunities of citizenship. It is now no more that toleration is spoken of as if it were by the indulgence of one class of people that another enjoyed the exercise of their inherent natural right, for happily, the government of the United States, which gives to bigotry no sanction, to persecution no assistance, requires only that they who live under its protection shall demean themselves as good citizens in giving it on all occasions their effectual support. May the children of the stock of Abraham who dwell in this land continue to merit and enjoy the good will of the other inhabitants, while every one shall sit in safety under his vine and fig tree, and there shall be none to make him afraid."

Religious Freedom under the Constitution

In no country of Europe, at the time of the birth of the American Republic, were church and state separated. The religion of the king was the official religion of the land. People not accepting the religion of the state were often persecuted. Catholic France persecuted the Huguenots, who were French Protestants. Catholics, Quakers, as well as such Protestant groups as Puritans, were persecuted in Protestant England, where another Protestant sect, the Anglicans, controlled the government. In some countries, people practicing a religion other than the state religion were "tolerated," as were the Jews in Holland, though they were not permitted to vote and hold office.

The United States became the first country where church and state were completely separated. In 1787 a conference of delegates from the thirteen states met in Philadelphia to draw up a set of laws for the new United States. After many months of work, the country's leaders drew up the Constitution with its Bill of Rights, guaranteeing religious freedom to all. "Congress shall make no law respecting an establishment of religion, or prohibiting the free exercise thereof," declared the first amendment to the Constitution of the United States.

One by one, the states ratified the Federal Constitution, some reluctantly, some amidst ringing bells and booming cannon. "Liberty throughout the land unto all the inhabitants thereof" became the law of the Republic.

But liberty throughout the land was a new idea to many people, not only in Europe, but even in the United States. There were not many states in the Union founded on the principle of complete equality for all. Roger Williams and William Penn had believed that the state had no right to interfere with the religion of its inhabitants. But these ideas were not shared by all the colonists. The New England colonies had their own state religion, a form of Protestantism. The

Carolinas and Virginia had set up the religion of the Church of England. Maryland had been set up under Catholic rule and gave freedom of religion only to Christians. Some of the colonies did not officially admit Jews. Some admitted them but denied them the right to vote and hold office.

Now, with the creation of the Federal Constitution guaranteeing religious freedom to all, men took up the fight in the separate states to follow the principle laid down by the central government, equal rights for all citizens, including the right to vote and hold office.

The First States to Guarantee Religious Freedom

Even before the adoption of the Federal Constitution, as early as 1777, the Legislature of New York State amended its constitution to guarantee religious freedom to all. Then came Virginia, where two future presidents of the United States, James Madison and Thomas Jefferson, led the struggle to wipe out discrimination because of religious beliefs. So proud was Thomas Jefferson of his role in the fight for religious freedom, that he wanted it recorded on his tombstone that he was the author of the Virginia Statute for Religious Freedom. Jefferson was ambassador to France when his bill was debated in the Legislature of his state. But James Madison and other supporters of the bill carried on the fight until it was finally won.

Other states, like Georgia, Pennsylvania, South Carolina, quickly followed the example of Virginia, Georgia in 1789, and Pennsylvania and South Carolina one year later. But in some states people clung stubbornly to their prejudices for many years.

In North Carolina

Jacob Henry was elected to the Legislature of North Carolina in 1808 and again in 1809. One of Henry's opponents tried to have him unseated on the ground that he was a Jew, and according to the constitution of North Carolina, only Protestants could hold office. Jacob Henry took up the fight. "Nothing is more easy to demonstrate," he said, "than that conduct alone is the subject of human laws, and that man ought to suffer civil disqualifications for what he does, and not for what he thinks. . . ."

Two Catholic office holders, as well as many other citizens who were opposed to religious discrimination, helped Jacob Henry in his fight. In the end, Jacob Henry was permitted to retain his seat. But it was not till after the Civil War, in 1868, that the law was officially amended to give religious liberty to all.

The Struggle in Maryland

It was a Scotch Presbyterian, Thomas Kennedy, who led the fight for religious freedom in Maryland. Since the constitution of Maryland granted religious freedom to all but Jews and atheists, there were very few Jews in Maryland. But Kennedy fought for the principle involved. He wanted the same right for others, he said, that he enjoyed himself. "There are few Jews in the United States," he declared in one of his speeches, "in Maryland there are very few, but if there were only one, to that one we ought to do justice. . . ."

Kennedy's bill to give the Jews complete equality came to be called the "Jew Bill." When he ran for office again, campaigning for his bill, he suffered defeat. But four years later, in 1826, Kennedy was re-elected to office, and the bill for which he had fought became the law of Maryland.

Questions to Discuss

Discuss Washington's statement: "It is now no more that toleration is spoken of as if it were by the indulgence of one class of people that another enjoyed the exercise of their inherent natural right, for happily, the government of the United States, which gives to bigotry no sanction, to persecution no assistance, requires only that they who live under its protection shall demean themselves as good citizens in giving it on all occasions their effectual support."

Why, after the revolution, did many people still resist the principle of equal rights for all?

Discuss Jacob Henry's statement, "Nothing is more easy to demonstrate than that conduct alone is the subject of human laws, and that man ought to suffer civil disqualifications for what he does, and not for what he thinks. . . ."

Things to Do

Pretend your class is a Jewish community living at the time of George Washington. Write him a letter of congratulations. Tell him something about your community, where you came from, what you hope will be the future of the United States.

Teachers Bibliography

Marcus, Jacob Rader, *Early American Jewry,* Volume Two.

CHAPTER 4

How Freedom Grew

The American colonists did not wipe their hearts clean of prejudice when they settled in the New World. They came with their old habits of thinking and their old habits of hating. Protestant was prejudiced against Catholic, Puritan against Quaker, this man against that. They came to a great wilderness of forests and mountains and valleys and plains and rivers. The land stretched for thousands of miles around, yet they found, as time went on, that there was no room for prejudice.

When men worked side by side putting up a stockade near a lonely forest, listening for the tread of the Indians or the whirr of an arrow, they did not ask one another whether they were Baptist or Jew or Quaker or Catholic. When the loaded pack trains of Michael Gratz followed the dark and winding Indian trails to the isolated frontiersmen waiting for supplies, the frontiersmen did not ask the drivers of the wagons the religion of the man who had sent them, before they accepted the food and clothes they needed to keep alive. When Isaac Cohen, a pioneer settler of Lancaster, came on a horse through snowdrifts and over frozen rivers to the home of a German farmer

to care for his ailing child, the worried farmer and his wife did not ask the good doctor whether he attended a church or a synagogue.

Slowly, in the wilderness of the New World, men grew to know one another. People travelled from many miles around to see Joseph Jonas, a Jew, who came from England and settled in the Ohio Valley. They came on foot and on horse to see what a Jew looked like, for they had never seen a Jew. An old Quaker woman turned him round and round. "Thou art no different from other people!" she cried at last in amazement.

In the populated towns, in the isolated settlements beyond the forest trails, at the far-flung outposts of the New World, on the busy wharves, men worked together and learned to respect one another, and slowly prejudice died. There were always men to show the way to freedom—Roger Williams, William Penn, Thomas Jefferson, James Madison, Benjamin Franklin, Thomas Kennedy. . . .

In the building of freedom, there is often a going forward, a sliding back, and a going forward again. Roger Williams, founding father of Rhode Island, insisted on religious freedom for all. But those who came after Roger Williams did not all follow in the path he had set. Aaron Lopez, Jewish resident of Newport, merchant prince, builder of his country, was denied citizenship in Rhode Island. But Aaron Lopez had learned that America was not Portugal. He had learned that in America a man could insist on his rights, as Asser Levy had done in New Amsterdam. A man did not knuckle under when a group of prejudiced city fathers denied him his due. Massachusetts, once intolerant of other people's religious beliefs, had moved forward in its concept of freedom. Aaron Lopez got into his carriage one day and drove over to Massachusetts, where he received his certificate of citizenship. Aaron Lopez, refugee from Portugal, was transformed into Aaron Lopez, proud citizen of the New World.

Freedom grew because men insisted that it grow. It spread, because its influence reached far and wide. It was only a short distance from Rhode Island to Massachusetts, a journey of a day or two over bad roads. So prejudice had to yield and freedom took its place, in the towns, on the farmsteads, in the taverns where men met over a tankard of ale, in the colonial kitchens where women sat spinning together.

In many lands of Europe the Jews were confined to ghettoes. In Russia, they could live only in a section of land called the Pale of Settlement.

In America a Jew lived where he pleased. Abraham Mordecai, a veteran of the revolution, struck out from Pennsylvania and founded Montgomery, Alabama.

In Europe Jews were barred from the crafts and from agricultural life.

In America a Jew did what he pleased. He could be a farmer, a snuff-maker, an inventor, a wig-maker, a candle-maker. Myer Myers was a silversmith. So skilled was he at his craft that he was elected president of New York's Gold and Silversmiths' Society.

In the Old World, few Jews were permitted to attend universities.

In America, the trustees of Rhode Island College, now Brown

University, declared that Jews would be admitted like all other students and allowed the freedom of their religion. Thomas Jefferson insisted that the University of Virginia, which he founded, have no official religion.

As freedom grew in America, its influence spread beyond the sea. The vessels shuttling back and forth across the Atlantic Ocean carried letters from the New World.

Jonas Phillips, a Jewish merchant of New York, sent a copy of the Declaration of Independence to a relative in Holland.

Solomon Simson and Alexander ben Zvi, also of New York, wrote a Hebrew letter to the Chinese Jews of Kaifung in 1795. "We in America, in New York and in other places, live in great security. Jews together with Gentiles sit in judgment on civil and criminal cases. . . ."

And the vessels carried stories of America's new way of life.

Peter Harrison, a Christian, had drawn up the architectural plans for the Newport synagogue.

In 1788 the Mikveh Israel congregation in Philadelphia needed money to keep going. Benjamin Franklin headed the list of contributors with five pounds.

In New York, Jews had contributed to the building of the steeple on Trinity Church.

A parade was held in Philadelphia to celebrate the ratification of the Constitution. Arm in arm with the priests and ministers of the city walked Jacob Raphael Cohen, rabbi of Mikveh Israel.

Gershom Seixas of New York was one of the trustees of Columbia College.

Farmer, ship owner, sailor, silversmith, wig-maker, carpenter, doctor, frontiersman, plantation owner, driver of the pack train, Catholic, Jew, Protestant, Quaker, Lutheran . . . they all grew to appreciate and respect one another in America. That is why freedom grew.

UNIT THREE BUILDING
JEWISH
LIFE

CHAPTER 1

Pioneers From the Germanic Lands

Upheaval in the Old World

As the United States expanded westward in the early half of the nineteenth century, more and more immigrants came to build its cities and turn its forestland into homesteads. Thousands upon thousands of artisans of the Old World, thrown out of work with the development of the machine, came to the New World to escape starvation. The spread of the ideals of freedom also brought waves of immigrants to the shores of America. The success of the American revolution had given the French people greater courage to throw off their monarchy and establish a republic. The success of the French revolution, in turn, roused in other oppressed peoples the hope of gaining freedom. Napoleon Bonaparte, leading the French armies through Europe, brought with him the slogan of the French revolution—liberty, equality, fraternity. Despite his despotism, Napoleon introduced many reforms into the lands he conquered. But when the French armies were defeated at Waterloo, in 1815, and Napoleon was banished to Elba, the monarchs returned to their thrones and tried to restore the old order.

But the old order could never again be completely restored, for the people had had a taste of freedom and many were ready to resist tyranny. Revolutionary underground movements developed, and when leaders of the movements were imprisoned, there were others to take their place.

The hungry peasant and craftsman, however, could not patiently wait till their rulers were overthrown. Tired of the wars that had torn Europe, longing for peace and security, many decided to come to America. In the years following Waterloo, they came in the hundreds of thousands from the Germanic lands. In 1848, revolution broke out in Austria and in other Germanic lands. But the rebellions were crushed, and again there was a wave of migration to America, this time made up of the "forty-eighters," as those who fled after the failure of the revolution of 1848 were called.

The Jewish Immigrants

For hundreds of years, the Jews of the Germanic lands had been forced to live in the dark, narrow streets known as *Judengassen,* or

ghettoes. With the coming of Napoleon, the ghettoes had been wiped out and emancipation seemed finally to have dawned. Some of the richer Jews sent their sons to the universities, hoping they would be able to enter the professions, like many of their Christian neighbors. The return of tyranny, however, brought an end to their hopes. But the glimpse of freedom they had had made them more dissatisfied than ever with the old life of oppression. Although they did not return to the ghettoes, they were still targets for attack. The poorer Jews in the small towns lived in dire poverty. In addition, they were heavily taxed, and special laws kept them from moving freely from place to place. Hemmed in, poor, weary of persecution, they grew impatient with the lives they lived and with the dreary future that lay before them and their children.

So thousands of them left their drab little villages and made their way to the seacoast cities, where they booked passage for America. Tailors, cobblers, dealers in second hand clothes, tinsmiths, sold their few possessions and left forever the villages where they had known only struggle and hardship. Often, despite all his saving and scrimping, a man did not have money enough to buy steamer tickets for the whole family. Then he went to America alone, saving all he could from his meager earnings till he had enough to send for his wife and children. Sometimes groups of friends went together, and sometimes a whole village was emptied of its Jewish inhabitants and only the old synagogue was left to mark the place where Jews had once lived and worshipped.

But there were many Jews who did not leave for America during the wave of migration following the year 1815. Some of the wealthier Jews, and those who had attended the universities, waited, hoping for better times, many of them working in the underground movement. When the rebellion of 1848 was crushed, however, they felt that all hope of freedom in their old homes was gone, and they joined the flight of the "forty-eighters" to the New World.

Opportunities in America

Most of the immigrants from the Germanic lands turned west, to
the Ohio Valley. On its green, fertile meadows, they built homes
and plowed the soil. But because the Jews had been prohibited from
owning land in the Old World and were therefore unaccustomed to
working on the soil, the majority naturally found their way to the
populated cities. Many of the "forty-eighters" went into business,
opened factories, or, if they had attended universities, were able to
enter some of the professions. But most of the Jewish immigrants
had neither money for business nor the education needed for entering the professions. Many of them learned a craft and became lens-
grinders, watchmakers, carpenters, tailors. Some became drovers,
shoemakers, brewers.

But still there were many who felt helpless and bewildered in the
large, bustling cities. Eager to earn a living quickly, thinking of
their families in the Old World who needed help or who waited for
money to pay their passage to America, they looked around for
something they could do at once, without skill or training. All
about them they saw wage-earners, the charcoal men, the scissors
grinders, the newsboys, porters, waiters, clerks, street cleaners, factory workers. But there were enough of these in the crowded cities.
They must go elsewhere, they realized, if they wanted to make a
living. But where, and what could they do?

Beyond the cities, in the western reaches of America, lay thousands of acres of farmland, virgin forests, green, fertile valleys.
Here and there, along the open stretches, far from cities and towns,
lonely settlements had gone up on riverbanks or beyond the forest
trails. No pack trains brought goods to the isolated farmers, and a
trip to the nearest town meant miles over bad roads or through forests. Getting goods was a hardship to the pioneer, isolated as he
was in the open spaces of America.

But the busy cities teemed with goods, goods from foreign lands and goods produced in the factories of America. The warehouses, the wholesale houses, the stores were piled high with goods beyond the reach of the pioneer. Many immigrants saw that here was a way to make a living, by bringing the goods from the cities to the pioneers pushing back the wilderness.

The Peddler

Thus many Jewish immigrants from the Germanic lands became peddlers. In a basket, or in a pack, or a trunk strapped to his back, the peddler carried his goods to the small villages and farms which the pack trains and steamers did not reach. Beyond the large cities he went, seeking out the tiny hamlets and isolated farmsteads. Following trails made by the pioneers, or blazing trails of his own, he

went westward, to the open country of Illinois, Ohio, Indiana, Mississippi, Missouri, Louisiana, Kansas, Nevada, Oregon. From farm to farm he trudged with his trunk or pack filled with calico, needles, pins, watches, lace, ribbons, tea, sugar, coffee. . . . When his pack was empty, he went back to the city, rested a day or two, bought more goods, then again made his way to the isolated settlements. Unfamiliar with the English language, he quickly mastered a few words that would help him make himself understood—good morning, good day, do you want to buy, I sell, thank you. . . .

Through rain, through snow, he plodded on through forests and over trails and highways, walking ten, twenty miles a day, often wondering where he would spend the night, wondering what his future would be in the land he had chosen to be his home. Some peddlers, like Isaac Bernheim, loved the life of freedom, the meeting with new people, the stretch of open road. Isaac Bernheim left his native land when he was eighteen, and coming to America, peddled in Pennsylvania. "The new avocation," he wrote years later, "afforded me many opportunities to familiarize myself with the language and customs of the people and with the country itself. . . . It developed me physically, and what was worth still more to me, it gave me a spirit of independence and self-reliance which stood me in good stead afterward . . . I trudged along the peaceful Pennsylvania highways dreaming of future triumphs. . . ."

But another Jewish peddler, Abraham Kohn, did not dream of triumphs as he trudged from farm to farm. Abraham Kohn came to New York City from Bavaria, and for ten months, his pack on his back, he sold his wares in the neighborhood of New England. Barely making a living, suffering hunger and cold, he wrote, in his diary, of his hard life in America, of his loneliness, of the icy nights spent in a wilderness far from friends and family. He complained too of the difficulty of observing his Jewish customs. The open field, he wrote, was often his house of prayer. But he consoled himself with a verse from the Bible, ". . . in every place where I cause My name to be mentioned I shall come unto thee and bless thee."

Abraham Kohn did not remain a peddler all his life. In 1842 he opened a store in Chicago, and years later entered the clothing business. A staunch abolitionist, he sent Abraham Lincoln a gift when the newly elected President of the United States was on his way to the White House. The gift was a flag of the United States with several verses from the Book of Joshua inscribed upon it. One of the verses read, "Be strong and of good courage."

Meyer Guggenheim, founder of the famous Guggenheim family, began as a peddler. Knowing little English, he trudged through the mining towns of Pennsylvania selling glue, stove polish, ribbons, needles, spices, lace. . . . Till the housewives grew to know him, they were wary of the stranger who could hardly make himself understood. But as time went by they looked forward to the monthly visits of the young peddler.

So it was with housewives all over the country. The peddlers broke the monotony of their lives. For not only did the peddler bring the goods they needed, but also the sparkle and glow of civilization, bits of gossip, anecdotes, news of the day, a glimpse of the big cities they longed to visit. Eagerly the pioneer family awaited his coming, both for the goods he carried in his pack and for the news he brought of the outside world.

The peddler lived frugally, buying only the bare necessities, saving all he could to bring his family to America. Then, with his family settled in the New World, he began to save again, this time for a horse and wagon to make his work easier. Sometimes, when a peddler came to a town or settlement where he felt he would like to live, he set up a small store and the farmers from far and near came to buy his goods. Louis Stix, who became a rich man, began as a pack peddler in Ohio and Indiana, then bought a horse and wagon. Later, with three partners, he opened a small store in Ohio. Some of the things he sold were sacks of sugar, twenty-eight pounds for one dollar, molasses at 18¾ cents a gallon, sheeting at 12½ yards for a dollar with a spool of thread and a card of hooks and eyes thrown in.

Lazarus Straus, one of the "forty-eighters," came from Bavaria and began as a "wagon peddler" in Georgia. He travelled from plantation to plantation, selling dry goods and "Yankee notions"— scissors, knives, ribbons, lace, watches, chinaware. . . . Like other peddlers who travelled through the southern states, Straus was always warmly welcomed by the plantation owners who looked forward to his periodic visits. And as was customary, he was invited to spend the night in the plantation manor. In the morning, before departing, he would give a gift to the lady of the house or to her daughter. In his wanderings through Georgia, Lazarus Straus came upon the town of Talbotton, with its neat houses and well-kept gardens. Here, he decided, he would like to live. With a partner, who was also a peddler, he rented a store which he stocked with goods bought on credit from friends in Philadelphia. Then, confident of the future, he sent for his family, his wife Sara, his sons Isidor, Nathan and Oscar, and his daughter Hermina.

As the towns of the country grew into cities, the general stores grew with them. Now and then a large department store developed from the stores of immigrant peddlers, stores like Altman, Bloomingdale, Gimbel Brothers. But most of the peddlers did not grow prosperous. They were happy to make a living, happy to return, after several weeks on the roads, to a warm home and the companionship of family and friends. Their dream was to settle down and open a store, some day, in a quiet town.

Many peddlers walked the trails, the lanes and the highways of America during the period of its expansion. For thousands of immigrants, Jews and Christians, took to peddling because they were unskilled. The open country was their school, where they learned to know the language, the customs, the people. Following in the wake of the pioneer, the peddler raised the American standard of living, making available the goods of the cities to the frontier settlements. In building his own economic life, the peddler helped America grow.

Things to Read

Rugg, Harold, *America: A Nation of Immigrants,* Ginn and Company, Boston, 1938.

Shippen, Katherine B., *Passage to America,* Harper and Brothers, New York, 1950.

Questions to Discuss

Compare the early Jewish settlers from Spain and Portugal with the Jewish settlers from the Germanic lands.

Compare the life of the Jews in the villages of the Germanic lands with their life in America.

Things to Do

Write the diary of a young Jewish immigrant from Bavaria covering his
first few months in the United States.

Start a project called "Our Jewish Community." Try to find out when
the first Jews came to your city. Who were they? Where did they come
from? What did they do to make a living and where did they worship?
Go on to later arrivals. Find out about their organizations, how they
differed from the earlier immigrants. You may want to form committees to investigate different aspects of your research.

Teachers Bibliography

Kisch, Guido, *In Search of Freedom,* Edward Goldston and Son,
    London, 1949.

Kraus, Adolf, *Reminiscences and Comments,* Toby Rubovitz, Chi-
    cago, 1925.

Learsi, Rufus, *The Jews in America,* pp. 58-78.

Wischnitzer, Mark, *To Dwell in Safety,* Jewish Publication Society,
    Philadelphia, 1948.

CHAPTER **2**

Changing Worlds

The Old Meets the New

Coming from the Old World to the New meant more than merely exchanging persecution for freedom. It meant learning how to earn a living, how to speak a new language and practice new customs. It meant keeping the old and cherished religion and its ceremonies in a strange and unfamiliar environment. The eager immigrant, peering anxiously at the buildings of the harbor city from the deck of the steamer bringing him to his new home, did not dream of the obstacles he must overcome before he could find his place in America.

The feeling of being part of America came slowly to most of the Jewish immigrants of the early nineteenth century. Surrounded by people who spoke a strange language, they looked for friends who would understand them, and who had the same background. They naturally drifted toward each other, finding security in praying together, in discussing their problems and their experiences in the New World.

The Early Synagogue

As soon as there were ten male Jews in a town, they formed a congregation so that they could hold services together. The first

121

Jews who came to what is now New York City founded the Shearith Israel congregation. These early settlers who had stemmed from Spain and Portugal were known as *Sephardim*. Later arrivals in New York, those coming from the Germanic lands and from eastern Europe, were known as *Ashkenazim*. The *Ashkenazim* had their own synagogue customs, their own way of pronouncing the Hebrew words, even their own way of chanting the prayers. But since they joined Shearith Israel, they naturally had to grow accustomed to the *Sephardic* way of worship, as did other *Ashkenazim* who joined early *Sephardic* synagogues.

As more and more immigrants came to America in the early and middle years of the nineteenth century, more and more *Ashkenazim* formed their own congregations. People who came from the same town preferred to form their own congregation rather than try to learn new ways of worship. They wanted to be with people who spoke and prayed as they did, and who had the same memories of the old home town where they had spent their childhood.

Sometimes a congregation grew rapidly. If it had a few rich men among its members it was able to rent a house of worship or even build one. More often the congregation grew slowly, and its members, who were tailors, peddlers, butchers, storekeepers, could not afford to rent a building. Often they met in private homes, or they rented a basement in someone's house, or a small store. The larger cities, like Boston and New York, soon had many little congregations tucked away in stores, factory lofts and private homes. The smaller towns sometimes had a congregation, but very often they had none. In the West, people sometimes waited for years before there were enough of them to form a congregation. And the building of a synagogue often took as many years more.

In the Ohio Valley, in the district which is now Cincinnati, a congregation was established as early as 1824. In 1836 the twenty-four members of Sons of Israel felt it was time to build a synagogue,

but since they could not afford to put up a building they decided to write to the older congregations in the East for help. "We are scattered through the wilds of America as members of the same family and faith," they wrote, "and we consider it our duty to apply to you for assistance in the creation of a House to worship the God of our forefathers. . . . There is not a congregation within five hundred miles of this city . . . for the last four or five years nothing was heard but the howling of wild beasts and the more hideous cry of savage men. . . ."

The Jews from the Germanic lands who found their way to the Ohio Valley did not join the older Sons of Israel, whose ritual of prayer was somewhat different from theirs. They formed their own congregation, so that they could worship in their own way, and still later arrivals established synagogues of their own.

Between Two Worlds

The little synagogues of the immigrants of the early nineteenth century were more than just places to pray. The peddler, returning from a weary round that had lasted for a week or two or three, eager to relax and spend some time with his friends, hurried off to his synagogue. There he found them all, Jacob, Reuben, Samuel, Jonah, Levi, Aaron. . . . All old friends, they greeted him warmly as he threw open the door and appeared among them.

After prayer there was time for a chat. They compared experiences. They aired their troubles. Reuben, a peddler, wanted to cross the border from Ohio into Indiana, but a license for peddling in Indiana cost one hundred dollars, and where was he to get the money? Levi, a tailor, had been saving money for a year, since the day he came to Ohio, and he still did not have enough money to send for his parents in Bohemia.

But they had problems besides the financial ones. America gave them freedom, they agreed. A man could get ahead, do as he liked. No path was closed to him. But, they complained, they were so busy making a living, learning the new ways, that there was time for nothing else. And their children wanted to be "real Americans." They were impatient with their parents and their old-fashioned habits. They wanted to read only English books. For that matter, there were few other books to read.

There had been many problems in the old country, but not the problem of Jewish education for their children. In their home towns, every boy went to *ḥeder* as a matter of course. In the American town where they had come to make their homes, they found no *ḥeder* for their sons, no teachers, no rabbis for the small congregations they formed. Very few congregations had rabbis, only those that were able to pay the salaries of learned rabbis from the old country. Sometimes one of the men, perhaps more learned than the rest, would act as *ḥazan,* leading them in their prayers. He might also act as teacher for their sons, teaching them to read the Hebrew prayers and perhaps translate a few sentences from the Bible. But there were some Jews so isolated in the vast reaches of America that they never saw another Jew. And they did the best they could to practice their own customs, hoping that more of their people would soon join them so that they could form a congregation.

It was not often that a small congregation of Jews had the good fortune to have a trained teacher of Hebrew come its way. In the year 1850, Leopold Mayer, an immigrant from one of the Germanic lands, came to Chicago. At that time, there were about two hundred Jews in the city. They clung together, Mayer related years later, in sorrow and in joy, each concerned about his neighbor. On his very first Friday night in Chicago he watched, with one of his brothers who had come to the city before him, at the bedside of a sick child. Since doctors were rare, in those days, Jewish congregations made it a duty for their members to take turns watching at the bedside of the sick.

Unlike the Jews of his native land, the Jews of Chicago, Mayer found, engaged in a variety of occupations. Some had dry goods and clothing stores. Some were engaged in the cigar and tobacco business. One had become a plumber, another a carpenter. And of course, there were peddlers, some carrying packs, some driving in wagons, all respected by their customers who awaited their arrival each season before laying in their supplies.

Leopold Mayer joined the Sinai Congregation, which had only twenty-eight paying members. The synagogue was on the third floor of a wooden building, and the narrow entrance was usually cluttered with goods belonging to the auctioneer who occupied the store below. The congregation had no rabbi, no teacher. Each man, said Mayer, was his own rabbi and teacher. But the congregation did have a *shoḥet* and a *ḥazan.* When Leopold Mayer felt it was high time for the children to receive some religious instruction, he

had a notice posted on the synagogue door stating that he was opening a religious school. In his school, the newly arrived teacher
taught both Hebrew and German, and it is told that the first boy in
Chicago prepared for *Bar Mitzvah* was taught by Mayer.

The Early Jewish School

Before the days of the public school system, some of the older,
well-established congregations in the larger cities had schools attached to their synagogues. Here general subjects as well as Jewish
subjects were taught. The Shearith Israel congregation in New York
opened the first Jewish school as far back as 1731, not long after
the synagogue was dedicated. The *hazan* also served as teacher, and
he taught the children the religious customs of their people, the
reading of Hebrew, the chanting of the prayers, and how to translate some verses from the Bible. Since this was before the days of
the public school, and the only school where a child could learn
general subjects was at a Christian parochial school, it was not long
before Shearith Israel requested its *hazan* to teach additional
subjects, Spanish, English, writing and arithmetic. The early Jewish schools, conducted by the synagogues, taught secular as well
as Jewish subjects. The Beth Ahabah school in Richmond was attended not only by Jewish children, but by Christian children as
well. But in many places where there was no Jewish school, parents
were forced to send their children to Christian parochial schools if
they wanted them to have a secular education. Often they sent them
with misgivings, fearing that they might become estranged from
their own religion.

When Lazarus Straus came to Talbotton and considered settling
there, he asked first whether there was a school for his children. On
being assured that there were splendid schools for both boys and
girls, he decided to settle there. Like the schools everywhere else,
the schools of Talbotton, which had a population of about eight or

nine hundred, were parochial. Reluctantly, because his was the only Jewish family in town, Lazarus Straus sent his children to the Baptist Sunday school. The instructor, who was a gunsmith, taught his pupils their letters and read them sections of the Hebrew Scriptures. But the children's Jewish education was not neglected. Lazarus Straus, who knew Hebrew and was well-versed in the Bible and in biblical literature, was sought out by the ministers. Some of them would come to dine at the Straus home when they came to Talbotton on their circuit, and often Lazarus Straus would translate portions of the Bible to them. Conversations with their father, and listening to the discussions he held with the ministers, was the main religious instruction the Straus children received in Talbotton.

The Beginning of Organizations

Steadily, the Jews grew more numerous as immigrants continued to come to the New World. The small congregations multiplied, while some became large with the passage of time. Many a peddler became a storekeeper and many a tailor became a factory owner. New synagogues were built and new Jewish day schools were opened. Each congregation, whether large or small, provided for its poor, visited its sick, took care of newcomers till they could find work. But with the steady stream of Jews to America, the small synagogues, and even the large ones, found that they could not care for the needs of their members as well as of the new immigrants.

Societies and lodges began to develop outside the synagogue. Men formed mutual-aid societies to help one another in case of illness or unemployment. In 1843, in the city of New York, twelve men decided to form a mutual-aid society, to be called *Bundes Brüder*. The small society became, in time, B'nai B'rith, with branches all over the country as well as in foreign lands. As it grew, its original purpose changed to meet the larger needs of the growing Jewish community of America. B'nai B'rith also became an edu-

cational and cultural agency. In 1913, it set up an Anti-Defamation League to protect the Jews when they were attacked or slandered. And to promote Jewish culture, it established the Hillel Foundation in the colleges and universities of the country.

Aside from the mutual-aid societies like B'nai B'rith when it was first founded, there were coal societies to provide coal for those who could not afford to buy it, *matzah* societies which provided the poor with *matzah* during Passover, loan societies which lent money without interest to those who needed it, and societies called *Hakhnasat Orḥim,* to care for the needs of newcomers and itinerant Jews.

Groups of Jews often got together to establish their own hospitals, so that their people could have *kosher* food in case of hospitalization. They established orphan asylums and homes for the aged. And because many of the immigrants wanted to meet socially and keep abreast of the times, they formed societies and reading circles where they could come together to dance, sing or discuss the books·

they had read. But the social societies and reading circles were not enough to satisfy the hunger of the immigrants for more knowledge. To help satisfy this hunger, an association called the Young Men's Hebrew Association was founded in the middle of the nineteenth century in the city of Baltimore, and from there it spread to other cities. Gradually, as the nineteenth century advanced, the Y's of the country, like the Jewish centers which developed at a later time, broadened their programs to meet the growing needs of the Jewish community. Activities for children were introduced. Not only Jewish studies, but music, art, lectures, concerts and social activities all helped make the Y's an important part of Jewish community life.

Facing the Future

The Jewish pioneers had become part of America, helping to build its cities and towns, its industries and professions. But they had not forgotten their own way of life. From the very beginning, when twenty-three Jews came to New Amsterdam in 1654 and faced a hostile, prejudiced governor, they had insisted on being part of the New World and on maintaining their Jewish way of life. As the years went by and more and more Jews came to America, their inner life continued to develop. Synagogues, schools, lodges, societies, reading circles, Jewish centers, Y's, hospitals, orphanages, homes for the aged—all became a part of the Jewish community of America.

But there were still many problems the Jews faced during the middle of the nineteenth century. Though they now had many synagogues, especially in the more populated parts of the country, the synagogues were not united. They still depended on the Old World for their scholars and rabbis. The societies to help the poor worked independently, though here and there Hebrew Benevolent Societies, which united the various organizations that cared for the poor, began to appear. Many Jews, isolated in small towns, had no place to worship, no schools for their children, no one to guide them. But in time leaders began to appear to bring them the unity they needed and to help them build the institutions that would strengthen and enrich the way of life they had brought with them to the shores of America.

Questions to Discuss

Compare the Jewish school of the eighteenth and early nineteenth century with the Jewish school of today.

Compare the social, cultural and philanthropic organizations of the Jews of the nineteenth century with those we have today.

Things to Do

Write to Alexander Arkatov, Alexark and Norsim, Inc., 156 N. Arden Boulevard, Los Angeles 4, California, for the filmstrip, "Ceremonial Objects of Judaism."

Expand your study of your Jewish community by doing some research on the various philanthropic, educational, religious, social institutions. Whenever possible, make a field trip, so that you can get first-hand information.

Do some research on the terms *Sephardic* and *Ashkenazic*.

Teachers Bibliography

Handlin, Oscar, *Adventure in Freedom,* pp. 38-58.

Marcus, Jacob Rader, *Memoirs of American Jews,* Volumes One and Two.

Lebeson, Anita, *Pilgrim People,* pp. 188-231.

CHAPTER **3**

Trail-Blazers

Like every other section of the population, the Jews participated in the march to the West. The people who had been oppressed in the Old World, told where they could live, what they could do to earn a living, were now free to go and do as they pleased. This chapter tells the story of how they did whatever had to be done to conquer the wilderness. The men mentioned in this chapter were not chosen because they were the most important of their time, but because they were typical of the Jewish pioneers who helped America grow.

Jacob Isaacson was a merchant in California. In the Old World he would have been cooped up in a small town. In America he was a trail-blazer. Jacob Isaacson left California and journeyed deep into Arizona, to the Santa Cruz Valley, where he traded with the Indians. Often he feared for his life, for there was no one with him and he was unprepared to defend himself in case of attack. "It was lonely in those times," he said. "On some days there would be little

or no travel, and at night I had only the stars to keep me company. . . ." Quietly, without fuss or fanfare, Jacob Isaacson showed the way for others to follow in the wilderness of Arizona.

On the Trans-American Building in San Francisco, there is a plaque commemorating the Yom Kippur services that forty Jewish pioneers conducted in a room above a store on September 26, 1849. For the Jews were there too, in California's Gold Rush, coming on horse, in wagon, by boat. All day they dug for gold, and when evening came, if there were ten of them, enough for a *minyan,* they met for prayer in a field or a tent or a shack. As soon as they could, they rented a store or a room above a store, where they could worship in the way of their fathers.

Sometimes a Jew was one of the first to come to a patch of wilderness. Others followed, and when the wilderness became a village or a town, it was often named for the early Jewish settler who had come in its pioneer days and helped it grow. So we have the towns of Mayer, Solomonsville, Levy, Newman, Altman, Altheimer. Or a canyon, like Rose Canyon, named for Louis Rose, near San Diego. Or a bluff, Weiss Bluff, named for Louis Weiss who came to Texas from Germany.

Because they could move freely through America, barred from no activity they chose to follow, Jews were found in every corner of the land, doing whatever their hearts desired. They were buffalo hunters, ranchers, distillers, ferrymen, newspaper editors, mayors, government agents, miners, explorers. Julius Meyer, who had a store in Omaha, traded with the Indians. Meyer had friends among the Indian chiefs, for they trusted him and considered him an honorable man. The Pawnee Indians adopted Julius Meyer, calling him Box-ka-re-sha-hash-ta-ka, or "curly headed white chief with one tongue." This meant that Julius Meyer was an honest man. He did not say one thing and mean another.

Another favorite with many Indians was Edward Kanter, whom they called Bosh-bish-gay-bish-gon-sen, which means firecracker. For Edward Kanter was an amazingly active man, even to his active Indian friends. He ran away from his home in Germany when still a lad, came to America as a stowaway on a French vessel, took to peddling, then to clerking in a drug store. One day Edward Kanter was experimenting with some chemicals. The chemicals exploded and blew up part of the drug store, and Kan-

ter had to start all over again. This time he became a waiter on
a steamboat. Now it was the steamboat that blew up, through no
fault of Kanter's, however, and he was forced to swim for shore.
After many adventures, Edward Kanter finally settled in Detroit,
where he opened a store. The Indians came to trade with him, and
often they would sit in a circle with their white-skinned friend and
smoke a peace pipe. Because Edward Kanter had mastered the languages of the Huron, Chippewa and Pottawatomie Indians, he was
able to tell them, in words they understood, about his adventures in
Europe and in America.

Carrying some burlap, a Jewish immigrant peddler, Levi Strauss,
met a miner one day. Strauss asked the miner whether he wanted
to buy some burlap. But the miner did not want burlap. What he
wanted and could not seem to get anywhere, he said, was a good
strong pair of trousers, strong enough to withstand the rough treatment they got in the mines. Levi Strauss and a Jewish immigrant
tailor got together and made trousers out of the burlap. The pockets
of the trousers were riveted with copper, so that they could bear the
weight of tools and ingots. The miners were delighted with their
burlap trousers. Everyone began to buy them, and Levi Strauss had
to open a factory to turn them out in great number. To this day,
people at work and at play wear Levis, the trousers named for Levi
Strauss.

Judah Touro, son of Isaac Touro of Newport, became one of the merchant princes of the United States. Settling in New Orleans while it was still the territory of France, Touro opened a store, buying goods in New England and having them shipped to him by way of water. His business grew as the country expanded, and Touro became a wealthy man, sending his goods to foreign lands and to the settlements of the Mississippi Valley. Touro disposed of his money as easily as he made it, contributing to hospitals, libraries, Jewish congregations, Christian institutions. When Judah Touro died, he was brought to Newport, where he was buried in the famous old burial ground. On his tombstone were engraved the words: "The last of his name, he inscribed it in the Book of Philanthropy forever."

Mordecai Noah, an important political figure in New York, serving at various times as judge, mayor, sheriff, never forgot the oppression his people suffered in the Old World. Mordecai Noah dreamed a dream of making America a land of refuge for all his people, a temporary Promised Land till they could go on to Palestine, their ancient homeland.

A good place to bring his people, thought Mordecai Noah, would be Grand Island, near the city of Buffalo. Since Noah had not enough money to buy the island, several friends helped him by investing in land on the island. Then Noah called upon all the Jews

of the world to gather on the Niagara frontier to participate in the
founding of Ararat, a city of refuge.

On the day of the dedication, on September 15, 1825, a grand
procession was held in Buffalo, with bands of music, United States
officers, state officers, craftsmen, deacons, wardens, Noah's fellow
masons in full regalia. . . . In the midst of the procession came Mordecai Noah, dressed in the robes of a judge—for he expected to
be judge of the re-established nation. The dedication was held in
the Episcopal church, where Mordecai Noah delivered a talk and
where the cornerstone of Ararat rested in full display. On the stone
were inscribed the words:

> Hear O Israel, the Lord our God, the Lord is One
> Ararat
> A City of Refuge for the Jews

But the Jews did not come to Ararat. And the cornerstone now
rests in a glass showcase of the Buffalo Historical Society.

Solomon Nuñes Carvalho was a photographer and an artist. He
was a quiet man, little dreaming of adventure till John Charles

Frémont invited him to join his expedition into the West as photographer. Carvalho went because he was an admirer of Frémont, like thousands of other Americans. The famous explorer had already made four expeditions to the West, but this time he went in search of a desirable route for a railway to the Pacific. Fortunately, Carvalho kept a diary, called *Incidents of Travel and Adventure in the Far West*. From his book we learn about the push of the expedition over rocky mountains, through valleys and desert heat, through white wildernesses of snow, over prairies teeming with buffalo, blacktail deer, antelope, through Indian territory and through land where no men had been before. Carvalho, born in Charleston, a city-bred man, learned to shoot buffalo on the run and to stand guard in hostile Indian country. He galloped through prairie fire and waded rivers and stood on a mountain for hours, waist deep in snow, to make a panorama of the mountain ranges around him. Like all others of the expedition, he suffered hunger and thirst and frostbite. Often there was no food for days, and the men became mere shadows of themselves. Not all the men survived the expedition. But Carvalho lived to tell the tale of exploration and discovery to millions of Americans who knew little of the vast continent they inhabited.

Uriah Phillips Levy, a captain in the navy, fought for the abolition of corporal punishment of sailors. The freedom-loving captain, who was an admirer of another freedom-loving American, Thomas Jefferson, presented a bronze bust of the Founding Father to the American government.

Joseph B. Strauss, an engineer, built the Golden Gate Bridge in California, the bridge, they said, which could not be built.

In Dayton, Nevada, Adolph Sutro, an engineer, made a tunnel in Mount Davidson from the Carson River to the Comstock Lode, a tunnel, they said, which could not be made.

Relieved of their bonds, Jewish pioneers dug into mountains, built cities, laid roads, paved wildernesses. They were justices of the courts, vintners, boatmen, teamsters, governors, writers, actors, miners, storekeepers, soldiers. They were a free people in a free world.

Things to Read

Blandford, Benjamin W., *Off the Capes of Delaware,* "Levy, the Lion-Hearted," pp. 233-253.

Leonard, Oscar, *Americans All,* "The Pioneer Railroader," pp. 145-151.

Levinger, Elma Ehrlich, *The Golden Door,* "The Lucky Stone," pp. 163-176.

Lurie, Rose G., *The Great March,* "He Frees His Slaves," pp. 142-149; "Who Will Build Ararat?" pp. 150-161.

Pessin, Deborah, *Giants on the Earth,* "Noah's Ark," pp. 89-94; "Judah Touro Spends a Day," pp. 95-113.

Questions to Discuss

How did the freedom America offered her pioneers result in enriching the country?

Things to Do

Send to the Commission on Jewish Education, Union of American Hebrew Congregations, 838 Fifth Avenue, New York 21, New York, for the filmstrip, "Judah Touro—Friend of Man."

Do a mural depicting Jewish contributions to American life. Add to your mural as your story continues.

Teachers Bibliography

Goldberg, Isaac, *Major Noah,* Jewish Publication Society, Philadelphia, 1936.

Huhner, Leon, *The Life of Judah Touro,* Jewish Publication Society, Philadelphia, 1946.

Lebeson, Anita, *Pilgrim People,* pp. 232-254.

Markover, Abraham B., *Mordecai M. Noah,* Bloch Publishing Co., New York, 1917.

Postal, Bernard and Koppman, Lionel, *A Jewish Tourist's Guide to the United States,* Jewish Publication Society, Philadelphia, 1954.

Civil War

The Issue of Slavery

Like the rest of the American population, the Jews were divided in their feelings about slavery. Some of the Jews who had come to the United States early in its history had become plantation owners. Since the southern planters required many slaves to take care of their large plantations, they wanted to keep their slaves. The great majority of the Jews, however, did not live on plantations, but in the northern cities and towns. Most of them did not take slavery for granted, as did the people of the South, but opposed it, especially the Jews from the Germanic lands who had come to find freedom in America. They were ready to take up arms to abolish the system that made one man the master of another.

The Freedom-Loving Rabbi

In the city of Baltimore, where the feeling for slavery ran high, Rabbi David Einhorn endangered his life by calling for its abolition. Rabbi Einhorn was warned many times that he must stop preaching and writing against slavery. But the abolitionist rabbi refused to keep silent. Finally, when a pro-slavery mob went rioting through the city, attacking people who had expressed themselves

as favoring abolition, friends and policemen urged Rabbi Einhorn
to display a Confederate flag on his house. But when Rabbi Einhorn refused to take steps to protect himself, a group of young men
from his congregation stationed themselves in his home to protect
him in case of attack. Finally the rabbi decided that he would take
his family to Philadelphia, where they would be away from danger,
and return to Baltimore himself to continue his agitation for abolition. In the dead of night, he conducted his family out of Baltimore, and after a dangerous journey, arrived in Philadelphia. Mar-
tial law, however, made it impossible for Rabbi Einhorn to return
home, and he remained in Philadelphia, where he carried on his
anti-slavery work.

A Champion of Slavery

The pro-slavery forces also had their champions among the Jews.
The most famous of these was Judah P. Benjamin, who served in
the cabinet of Jefferson Davis. Benjamin, representing Louisiana in
the United States Senate, left Congress when his state seceded from
the Union. When the southern states established their own govern-

ment with Jefferson Davis as its chief, Judah Benjamin became Attorney General, then Secretary of War, and finally Secretary of State.

As Secretary of War, Benjamin was often under attack when things did not go well in the South. He was once asked to send arms to a post which was under fire by Union soldiers. Since he had no arms to send, the post was lost. When he was attacked for the loss of the post, Benjamin said nothing in his own defense, for he did not want it known that the southern troops were suffering a shortage of ammunition. But Jefferson Davis, who knew the truth of the matter, expressed his confidence in Benjamin by promoting him to the position of Secretary of State.

After Lee's surrender, Benjamin fled to England, never again to set foot in the United States. The brilliant statesman was often referred to by the people of the South as the "brains of the Confederacy." But Daniel Webster, a northern abolitionist, called him "an Israelite with Egyptian principles."

The Battle of Words

Unwittingly, a rabbi in New York City, Rabbi Morris Raphall, stimulated a battle of words on the question of slavery. Rabbi Raphall was asked whether, according to the Bible, slavery was permissible. The rabbi replied that it was. But, he went on to explain, the laws of the Bible prohibited cruelty to slaves, and the ancient Hebrews treated their slaves like human beings.

Feelings were running high at the time Rabbi Raphall made his statement, and his words were not carefully examined. Because he did not condemn the system of slavery, he was accused of supporting it. Jewish students of the Bible wrote articles to show that Rabbi Raphall had misunderstood the spirit of the Jewish law. Michael Heilprin, who had taken part in the Hungarian revolution of 1848 and who was widely known for his scholarship, maintained that it was wrong to suppose that the laws of Judaism were rigid and inflexible. Slavery may have been accepted as natural in ancient days, but what had applied to the civilization of an ancient people did not necessarily apply to a modern society.

At about this time a Jewish scholar of Copenhagen, Dr. Moses Mielziner, who later became a rabbi in New York City, wrote a book called *Slavery among the Ancient Hebrews*. Christian abolitionists in America, eager to have so scholarly a champion on their side, printed Dr. Mielziner's book in serial form so that it would reach wide audiences. Considering the time in which they lived, said Dr. Mielziner, the Hebrews were an advanced people in regard to slavery. For though slavery was taken for granted everywhere else in the civilizations surrounding them, the laws of the Jews tried to limit slavery, with a view to gradually abolishing it completely.

Heroes of the Civil War

Again, as in the war of the revolution, Jews from all over the land took up arms in defense of freedom. Since there were too many

to list, a chosen few will speak for all their comrades, for both the remembered and the forgotten ones.

Elias Leon Hyneman was a sergeant of the Fifth Pennsylvania Cavalry. He fought in the Battle of Bull Run, Gettysburg, and in the Battle of the Wilderness. Once, when his horse was shot from under him, he went on fighting on foot. When his term of enlistment was over, Hyneman re-enlisted. During a cavalry sortie near Petersburg, with the enemy hot on his heels, he dismounted to pick up a wounded comrade. He was continuing on to his own lines, when again he saw a wounded comrade, this one barely able to hobble along because he had no boots. Dismounting once more, Hyneman offered the wounded soldier his boots. Meanwhile the enemy closed in. Elias Leon Hyneman was captured and imprisoned. He died in prison of starvation and illness.

Leopold Newman was a Lieutenant-Colonel. When the term of his service expired, he remained on to fight in the Battle of Chancellorsville. During the battle he was badly wounded, and a short time later, he died in a hospital near Washington.

Max Sachs, a lieutenant in Company C of the Thirty-Second Infantry, performed one of the most heroic deeds of the war. He retarded the progress of the enemy, by whom he was surrounded, till his comrades could get the help they needed to carry on the battle. This happened in Bowling Green, Kentucky, where Max Sachs was killed in action.

Leopold Karpeles was Color Sergeant in Company E of the Fifty-Seventh Massachusetts Infantry. He was wounded, but insisted on rejoining his regiment though he had to use a cane. In the Battle of the Wilderness, his general entrusted him with the colors. Through a hail of enemy bullets, Karpeles stood firm, rallying the troops who were retreating in disorder, and thus saving a part of the army from being captured. Leopold Karpeles was awarded a medal of honor for his heroism.

Leopold Blumenberg enlisted after the attack on Fort Sumter, helping to organize the Fifth Regiment of Maryland Volunteers, of which he was appointed Major. Blumenberg served in many battles, till he was shot in the thigh while commanding his regiment in the Battle of Antietam. Because he was unable to serve in the forces, President Lincoln appointed him Provost Marshal of the third Maryland District. Later, President Johnson promoted him to the rank of Brigadier-General, U. S. Volunteers. But Blumenberg did not enjoy civil life for long. He died of the wounds he had received on the field of Antietam.

Benjamin Levy was sixteen years old when he enlisted as drummer boy in the First New York Volunteers. Levy was aboard the boat *Express,* carrying dispatches for his general, when it was attacked by a rebel gunboat. To confuse the enemy, Benjamin Levy cut loose a water schooner attached to the *Express.* The schooner was captured, while the *Express,* with all aboard, was saved. Later, in a southern battle, Levy's tent mate fell ill. To save him from being captured, Levy put aside his drum, took his comrade's gun and went out to fight with his regiment. During the battle he saved two of the regiment's colors, and for this act of bravery, was promoted to Color Sergeant of the Regiment. His two years of service ended, Levy re-enlisted in the Fortieth New York Regiment, and while fighting in the Battle of the Wilderness, he was wounded and left on the battlefield, where he remained for two weeks without shelter. But the tide of battle turned, and Levy was rescued by Union soldiers. For his gallantry, he received the Congressional Medal of Honor.

Edward Solomon joined the Twenty-Fourth Illinois Infantry as Second Lieutenant. Because of gallantry in action, he rose to the rank of Major. Later, Edward Solomon resigned to help organize the Eighty-Second Illinois Infantry, of which he became Colonel. Always remaining cool under fire, holding his lines under fierce assault, his gallantry was rewarded when he became Brigadier-General.

Father Abraham

To most of the Jews, the tall, gaunt President in the White House
seemed like a kindly father. Many of them, coming from a childhood of poverty, felt strong bonds with the man who had risen from
the backwoods to become President of the United States. Also,
Abraham Lincoln was like their own Moses of biblical days, the
emancipator who had led them from slavery. Since most of the
Jews hated slavery, Lincoln was a President in their own image.

Time and again the Jews of the country turned to the President
for help. Each time, Father Abraham gave them the help they asked
for. It happened once that General Ulysses S. Grant, acting before
he had thought the matter through, issued an order which reflected
the prejudice many people still had against the Jews. Grant had had
a series of victories in the neighborhood of Kentucky, Tennessee,
and in Mississippi. Hard on the heels of the victors came many
merchants, a few of them Jews, to buy cotton from the enemy
plantation owners. When Grant heard that northern merchants were
trading with the enemy, he assumed that the greatest number were
Jews, and he issued an order expelling the Jews from the territory.

The order was made public and the expulsion began. From all
over the country, from Jews and Christians, came a storm of protest against Order Number 11. From Paducah, in Kentucky, a committee of Jews set out to see the President. At the head of the committee was Cesar Kaskel. The President received Kaskel upon his
arrival and listened carefully to the tale he had to tell. Then Abraham Lincoln said, "And so the Children of Israel were driven from
the happy land of Canaan?" "Yes," replied Cesar Kaskel, "and that
is why we have come unto Father Abraham's bosom, asking protection." "And that protection they shall have at once," said Lincoln.

Then the tall, gaunt man with the haggard face sat down at his
desk and wrote a note to the General-in-Chief of the army, directing

him to have Grant's order revoked at once. The order was revoked, and the storm it had created died down. When Grant ran as the presidential candidate of the Republican party, however, people remembered Order Number 11, and Grant said he regretted what he had done. As President of the United States, Grant proved that his apology was sincere, for he was always friendly to the Jewish people.

It was April 14, 1865. The nation was celebrating the end of the Civil War. In Jewish synagogues and homes, Passover too was being celebrated. That night, as he sat watching a play in Ford's Theatre, in Washington, Abraham Lincoln was shot. The next morning, the American emancipator was dead.

The news flashed through the country, and the millions of people who had grown to love the great-hearted President wept with grief. The altars in the synagogues were draped with black as the day of rejoicing became a day of sorrow. Rabbis tried to console their grief-stricken congregations. In the Shearith Israel synagogue in New York City, a memorial prayer was offered for the first time for a man who was not a Jew.

Abraham Lincoln's body lay in state in the Court House of Chicago. Shielding him was a canopy, and upon it were inscribed words from the Bible, from David's lament over King Saul: "The beauty of Israel is slain upon the high places."

Things to Read

Alofsin, Dorothy, *America's Triumph,* "A Gift and an Opportunity," pp. 37-62; "Fight for Justice," pp. 63-92.

Blandford, Benjamin W., *Off the Capes of Delaware,* "A Million Pounds Sterling," pp. 282-296.

Leonard, Oscar, *Americans All,* "They Were Friends of Lincoln," pp. 114-122; "The Brains of the Confederacy," pp. 123-130.

Levinger, Elma Ehrlich, *The Golden Door,* "Behind the Stove," pp. 177-180; "The House of Bondage," pp. 181-187; "A Present From Mr. Lincoln," pp. 188-198.

Questions to Discuss

What did Daniel Webster mean when he called Judah P. Benjamin "an Israelite with Egyptian principles?"

Why were the great majority of the Jewish immigrants from the Germanic lands opposed to slavery?

Things to Do

Write an imaginary dialogue between Moses and Abraham Lincoln.
Collect all the Negro spirituals you can that have biblical themes. Discuss the ideas in the spirituals.

Teachers Bibliography

Korn, B. W., *American Jewry in the Civil War,* Jewish Publication Society, Philadelphia, 1951.
Learsi, Rufus, *The Jews in America,* pp. 90-110.
Lebeson, Anita, *Pilgrim People,* pp. 255-295.

CHAPTER 5

Builders of Judaism

Orthodox, Reform and Conservative Judaism

The movement of Reform Judaism had its beginning in the Germanic lands, after the defeat of Napoleon and the return of oppression and tyranny. Many young Jewish men and women, at this time, tired of being discriminated against because they were Jews, secking the freedom and opportunities which were denied them because of their religion, left the faith of their fathers and became Christians. It was then that a number of Jewish leaders, hoping to keep their young people true to their own faith, began the movement known as Reform Judaism. They felt that by modernizing and beautifying the synagogue and by changing some of the old customs, their youth would find their own synagogues as attractive as the churches they sought.

For centuries back, the Jews had accepted the Talmud as the highest authority. They had lived according to the *Shulḥan Arukh,* which was a summary of all the Jewish laws, those in the Talmud and those which were later developed. The leaders of Reform Judaism believed that the Talmud and the *Shulḥan Arukh* were no longer binding upon the Jews, and that many Jewish laws observed by their forefathers were no longer necessary. Each generation, they said, must give its own interpretation of Judaism. Some of the prayers, said the Reform leaders, should be in German, the language all the people understood, rather than in Hebrew, a language no longer understood by many Jews. To silence their enemies, who insisted that they were "different" and therefore not loyal Germans, the Reform leaders suggested that the passages in the prayerbooks referring to the Messiah and a return to Zion be eliminated. As for the synagogue, which the Jews through the ages had used not only as a house of worship but also as an informal gathering place where they chatted, studied, discussed their daily affairs, the Reform leaders tried to make it a solemn house of prayer, its dignity and beauty enhanced with choir and organ music.

But Reform Judaism had many opponents. The Orthodox Jews believed that the Torah was given to the Jews by God on Mount Sinai. Therefore, they said, every word was holy. When the realities of life and Torah came into conflict, it was the realities of life that must yield, for the Torah, being God's will, was unchanging. The Talmud and the *Shulḥan Arukh,* which were extensions of the Torah, must always remain the official law. No law, said the leaders of Orthodox Judaism, must ever be revoked.

Opposed both to Orthodox and Reform Judaism stood Conservative, or, as it was also called, Historical Judaism. Leaders of Conservative Judaism were opposed to Orthodox Judaism because they felt it was unyielding, and therefore contrary to the spirit of Judaism, which had always been flexible. They opposed Reform Judaism as well because they felt it was breaking with many ideas basic to Judaism. Leaders of Conservative Judaism did not believe in breaking with the past. But since Judaism was a living, developing organism, it naturally could not remain unchanged. Development, said the leaders of Conservative Judaism, involved change, but the changes must come within the continuity of Jewish life. Prayer, they said, had taken the place of sacrifice, and the synagogue had replaced the Temple. These changes however, had taken place without interrupting the historical development of Judaism.

But Hebrew was regarded as the holy language, the language of the Bible. Hebrew, they said, must therefore remain the language of prayer. The idea of Zion and of the Messiah had also become basic to Judaism, and this idea too could not be uprooted from the hearts of the Jewish people.

In the early period of Jewish history in America, all the Jews followed traditional Judaism, with slight differences, here and there, in the ceremonies and ritual of the synagogue. But in the course of time, three distinct types of Judaism took root, Orthodox, Reform and Conservative.

The Young Champion

Isaac Leeser came to Richmond from his native land of West-phalia in 1824. The eighteen year old youth had an uncle in Richmond, and to earn a living, he entered his uncle's mercantile business as a clerk.

But it was not really business young Leeser was interested in. He devoted his evenings to studying and reading, and whatever time he had left he spent in assisting the rabbi of the community, teaching the children and conducting services in the synagogue.

Four years went by, and Isaac Leeser was still in Richmond, an unknown young man working for his uncle, quietly devoting himself to his books and to the affairs of the community. Then suddenly Isaac Leeser became famous. Reading, in an English magazine, a series of articles slandering Judaism, he took pen in hand and wrote a series of his own articles defending his people and their religion. Though the articles were printed in a small local newspaper, *The Richmond Whig,* they attracted wide attention, and the following year the young champion was invited by the Mikveh Israel congregation of Philadelphia, one of the oldest in the country, to become its minister, or *ḥazan.*

Isaac Leeser was reluctant to leave Richmond for a city he did not know, but his uncle persuaded him to accept the post in Philadelphia, and he set out to take up his new duties in the historic city. There he lived for the rest of his life, becoming one of the outstanding leaders of American Jewry.

Beginning His Life Work

Isaac Leeser saw clearly what the Jews of America needed— more Jewish schools, more synagogues, academies for training rabbis, books, periodicals. All these they had had in the Old World, where they had taken many centuries to develop, and the Jewish community of the New World, like the New World itself, was still young. But Leeser felt that the growth of American Jewry's institutions should not be left to chance. Though shy and retiring by nature, he gave himself the difficult task of rousing his people to the need for uniting their forces to strengthen their way of life.

The *ḥazan* of Mikveh Israel felt that the day school, where children, both boys and girls, would pursue their Jewish as well as secular studies, must become part of every Jewish community. He felt that the Jews of America must stop depending upon the Old World for their rabbis and scholars, but must establish their own acadamies of learning. All the needs of American Jewry, Leeser felt, could be met if the congregations united, instead of trying to work out their problems alone.

To reach as many people as possible, Leeser founded a magazine, the *Occident*. In his periodical, he brought to his readers news of what was happening to Jews all over America as well as news about Jews in other parts of the world. Tirelessly, he travelled from city to city, from town to town, doing the pioneer work of organizing the Jews of America. He visited small groups of Jews and large groups, he dedicated synagogues, delivered sermons, appealed for unity of action. And after each trip, when he returned to Philadelphia, he wrote reports of what he had seen for the *Occident,* so that his readers would have a picture of what was happening in communities other than their own.

From the Pages of the "Occident"

When the *ḥazan* of Mikveh Israel went to Norfolk, Virginia, in the autumn of 1845, he was glad to find that the few Jews living there had acquired a *Sefer Torah,* and that they had gotten together during the high holydays for prayer. Moreover, Leeser reported in the *Occident,* one of them had volunteered to act as *shoḥet*. Twice a week he would slaughter cattle and fowl and the group would at last have *kosher* meat in their homes.

At Petersburg, Leeser found only a few Jewish families, not enough for a congregation. But in Richmond, where he had lived with his uncle when he first came to America, there were two congregations, one made up of *Sephardim,* Spanish-Portuguese Jews, and the other of *Ashkenazim,* Jews of western and eastern Europe. The minister of the *Ashkenazim,* Max Michelbacher, told Leeser that he intended to give his sermons in English rather than in German. Leeser agreed that this was an excellent idea. The Jews, he said, must adjust their customs to the conditions about them, and since English was the language of America, it was desirable that sermons be delivered in English.

There were other good bits of news Leeser had to report. He found that there were enough Jews in Wheeling, Virginia, to form a small congregation. And the Jews of Columbia, South Carolina, were framing a constitution for their new congregation.

In the fall of 1847, Isaac Leeser visited New York. Here he found that the women of Shearith Israel had formed a Ladies' Sewing Association. The women planned to meet every Wednesday during the winter months, from eleven to two o'clock, to sew clothes for the poor. Leeser hoped that they would clothe the poor in the summer and spring as well as in the winter.

The Reverend Jacques Lyons, minister of Shearith Israel, Leeser told his readers, had learned that the funds of the Hebrew Benevolent Association of New Orleans were exhausted. There had been a terrible epidemic in New Orleans, and the city had been desolated. Reverend Lyons went around to the members of his congregation and collected four-hundred and sixty-nine dollars, which he sent to Isaac Hart, president of the Hebrew Benevolent Association of New Orleans. Why, Isaac Leeser asked, had not the Jews of Philadelphia been notified that the Hebrew Benevolent Association of New Orleans needed money? They too would have been happy to contribute had they known that help was needed.

That year Isaac Leeser found many things to please him in New York. He liked the day school at Shearith Israel, and the one attached to Rabbi Max Lilienthal's synagogue. In Dr. Lilienthal's school he found one hundred and sixty students and four teachers. The children studied Hebrew translation and reading, geography, English, German. Leeser had a suggestion to make to the managers of the school. They must have the classrooms handsomely plastered and white-washed, he said. A fine, open room, Leeser told them, was a wonderful incentive to a scholar.

Leeser also founded a new literary society in New York. It was made up of German Jews, and they met every evening at eight o'clock to read and discuss the books and articles they had read. The Reform congregation, B'nai Emanuel, Leeser reported, had bought a church which they intended to convert into a synagogue.

In the spring of 1850 Isaac Leeser made a trip to New Orleans. The Jews of Spanish-Portuguese extraction had a synagogue at last. The building had served as a church, and when the Christian congregation built itself a new structure, Judah Touro bought the building and turned it over to the Jewish congregation. The congregation had then sent to Jamaica for a minister, Moses Nathan, and had invited Isaac Leeser to attend the consecration of the new synagogue. Now there were three organized Jewish groups in New Orleans, Isaac Leeser wrote. The Spanish-Portuguese group was the first to acquire a synagogue, but the other groups, he hoped, would not be far behind.

In the winter of 1851 Isaac Leeser visited the city of Louisville. Here he was invited to deliver a sermon by the Adath Israel congregation. Adath Israel had a beautiful new building for its synagogue, and the seats were filled when the visiting *hazan* delivered his sermon. But there was something to mar the pleasure of Leeser's visit. He did not see why the Jews who stemmed from Poland should have left Adath Israel, whose members were now all of German extraction, to form a congregation of their own. Why, Leeser asked, could not the two groups worship together, especially since their way of worship was almost the same?

The year 1853 found Leeser in New York again. This time he found seventeen congregations. Leeser suggested that if the congregations got together by instituting an annual conference, so that the heads of the congregation got to know one another, they could have unity of action whenever it was necessary.

The cornerstone of the Jews' Hospital of New York (now Mount Sinai) was laid on November 24th, 1853, Leeser reported in his journal.

In 1856, Leeser found that the number of Jews in Easton, Pennsylvania, had increased, and that the synagogue was not large enough to hold them all. He was sorry to learn, he reported, that the parents of the children attending the day school insisted that German be the vehicle of instruction. This is all wrong, said Leeser. The language of the country is English, and this should be employed, although German might be added as an accomplishment, like French and other languages.

Sowing the Seeds

So year after year Leeser travelled, delivered sermons, dedicated synagogues, called for union of the congregations of America. Patiently, he educated the people he met, preparing the soil for the seeds he and others were to sow.

In time, Leeser came to be considered the leading spokesman for the Jews of America. He wrote text books for children, organized the Board of Delegates of American Israelites, the first union

Mikveh Israel Synagogue in Philadelphia.

of Jewish congregations of America. Gradually, he built up a following of men who were ready to work with him. With the help of
his supporters, he founded the Jewish Publication Society to publish books on Jewish subjects, the first publication house of its kind
in the New World. Knowing that many Jews no longer read Hebrew, he translated the Bible into English and produced prayerbooks in Hebrew and in English both for the *Sephardic* and the
Ashkenazic congregations.

Among the worshippers at Mikveh Israel was the famous Michael
Gratz family. Rebecca Gratz, the daughter of Michael, realized that
there was need for providing some religious instruction for the Jewish children of Philadelphia. Guided by Isaac Leeser, who prepared
the material used in the school, she organized a Jewish Sunday
school, the first in the country.

Fearing that many Jewish children would be alienated from their
own faith if they attended Christian parochial schools, Leeser used
his magazine to spread the idea of the Jewish day school. The day
school, he felt, should be connected not only with one congregation, but should be the responsibility of the whole Jewish community. In 1848, Leeser organized the Hebrew Education Society, a
day school which he hoped would serve the entire Jewish community of Philadelphia.

Leeser hoped that in time the Jews of Philadelphia would establish a higher school of Jewish learning for educating rabbis and
other leaders. He did not feel, however, that the time was ripe for
such a project, so he did not speak of it openly. But he gave expres-
sion to this hope by including, in the charter for the Hebrew Education Society, the right not only to establish and maintain elemen-
tary Jewish schools, but also the right to establish a college which
would be authorized to grant college degrees.

Years passed. Leeser went on agitating for a higher Jewish school
of learning. Finally, in 1867, it seemed that Leeser's fondest dream
was to come true. In that year, Maimonides College, the first col-

lege in the country for the training of rabbis, opened in the city of Philadelphia. Leeser, who became president of the college, also joined the small staff of scholars he had recruited to teach the students. But Leeser's hopes were not realized. He had wanted Maimonides College to be a national institution, supported by Jews from all over the country. The college, however, was supported by only a handful of Jews in Philadelphia, and in 1873, a few years after Leeser's death and only six years after it was founded, lack of funds forced Maimonides College to close its doors.

But the seeds had been sown. The idea of a college continued to grow. In time, other colleges were opened to train rabbis and scholars for the Jewish community of America.

The Rabbi From Bohemia

One day in July, in 1846, a young rabbi arrived in New York City with his wife, his young child, and two dollars in his pocket. Isaac Mayer Wise had dreamed of coming to America ever since he had wandered into a bookstore in Prague, one day, and bought some old American newspapers. The newspapers had contained debates on the Federal Constitution, and sitting in his study with the yellowed journals spread before him, Isaac Mayer Wise had had a glimpse into the New World with its many opportunities for Jews and Christians alike. Taking his wife and child he had gone to Bremen without a passport, and after a long voyage lasting sixty-three days, had finally set foot upon the shore of the New World.

Like Isaac Leeser, Isaac Mayer Wise, too, saw the chaos about him, the small Jewish communities, each going its own way, the lack of schools, the need for American-born rabbis. Despite the fact that many of the aims of Isaac Leeser and Isaac Mayer Wise were the same and the two men tried, several times, to work together, they finally were forced to pursue different paths to reach their goals. For unlike Leeser, Rabbi Wise believed in Reform Judaism. Although there were several Reform congregations in America when Rabbi Wise arrived, the movement was still weak. But with the coming of Wise it began to spread, for it had found, in the young rabbi from Bohemia, a strong and determined leader.

Isaac Mayer Wise began his work in Albany, where he became rabbi of a small Orthodox congregation. Gradually, he began to introduce changes in the synagogue service, a choir of mixed voices, sermons in the English language. Using the lower story of the house he lived in for classrooms, Wise opened a day school, and with two assistants to help him, took over the education of the children of the congregation.

But things did not go smoothly for the Reform rabbi. Although some of the members of the congregation favored the changes in the synagogue service, many opposed them, and at last the opposition grew so strong that Rabbi Wise felt he must resign if he was to carry on his work. His supporters followed him and together they founded a new Reform congregation.

Leader of Reform Judaism

Wise spent eight years in Albany, and during that time he came to be recognized as the leader of Reform Judaism in America. But as strong as his hope that the Reform movement would spread, was his hope that the congregations would unite. Combining their forces, Leeser and Wise worked together for unification, Leeser working in Philadelphia, in the West and in the South, and Wise working in the East. The efforts of the two leaders, however, ended in failure. The congregations were still not ready for union. Undismayed, Wise continued working, writing articles, visiting congregations, preaching, explaining the aims of Reform Judaism, agitating for a rabbinical college.

In 1853 Wise received an offer from the B'nai Jeshurun congregation in Cincinnati to become its rabbi for life. "Now I began to ponder," Rabbi Wise later wrote in his *Reminiscences.* "What does Providence wish me to do? The temple and the congregation here are built up and firmly established. My mission here is ended. Anyone else can finish the work. . . . Cincinnati lies in the center of the country. There in the West is a new world that comes into but little contact with the east. . . . Now I understand what I have to do. I shall go to Cincinnati, start a new weekly journal, give Judaism a new and powerful impetus. . . ."

So Rabbi Wise went to Cincinnati, and from the time of his arrival, Cincinnati became the center of the Reform movement in the United States.

To reach both the English-speaking and the German-speaking Jews of the country, Rabbi Wise founded two magazines, *The Israelite,* written in English, and *Die Deborah,* written in German. But even with his publications, progress toward his goals continued to be slow. The fighting, determined rabbi pushed ahead, however, despite discouragement and setbacks.

Reminiscences of Rabbi Wise

Rabbi Wise had expected the publication of *The Israelite* to be an easy matter. "A number of friends," he wrote, "had promised me original contributions and translations; but when the campaign was ready to be opened, I found myself without an army. My sorriest embarrassment lay in the fact that I had announced Jewish novels in the prospectus, and could not obtain any. I wished to re-awaken the slumbering patriotism by Jewish stories and thus overcome the indifference. I had an object, therefore, in desiring novels, but despite all promises I had none. I had no choice but to write novels by the sweat of my brow. . . .

"A still greater difficulty lay in procuring readers. . . . No one was used to reading a Jewish paper. My personal friends read the paper and sought to circulate it; but their number was, sad to say, very small. . . ."

But Rabbi Wise went ahead with his publication, and gradually the circulation increased. *The Israelite* and *Die Deborah* reached into more and more homes, bringing to the Reform leader an ever-growing audience. Often Wise took trips, to lecture, to dedicate synagogues, to carry his message into the more isolated communities. In 1855 he was advised by his doctor to leave the city and take a trip for his health. He was distressed to find, as he stopped off at one town after another, that there were few congregations in the West, little interest in Judaism, and no Jewish leaders.

"I left the city at the end of July," he wrote, "and went to St. Louis by way of Indianapolis and Terre Haute. There was not a Jewish congregation between Chicago, St. Louis, and Cincinnati. . . . I found a number of acquaintances in Quincy . . . but no Jewish congregation. . . . The same condition of affairs prevailed in all towns on the Mississippi. . . . I saw everything, and became acquainted with everyone; but withal I longed to get back into the territory of Jewish civilization. . . . I arrived at Chicago on Thursday afternoon. . . .

"Chicago scarcely deserved to be called a city at that time. But the beginnings were there. A sea of little wooden houses, spread over an extended territory, badly paved streets, and wooden sidewalks, with a few handsome buildings—this was Chicago. It looked like an aggregation of a hundred adjoining villages. Signs with the warning, "Bottomless," appeared where now are some of the principal streets. These signs indicated swampy ground. A wagon mired there could not possibly be drawn out.

"There were two Jewish congregations in Chicago; one German, the Anshe Maarab; the other Polish. The synagogue of the former was a large wooden building; the latter worshipped in rented quarters. Ramah Lodge, I.O.B.B., and a small number of small societies were in existence; but there was nothing else, neither school nor charitable organization. . . ."

In Milwaukee, where Rabbi Wise spent several days, he found little interest in Judaism. "Such as were still faithful to the religion would have been sufficient, as far as number, intelligence, and wealth went, to form a respectable congregation; but in lieu thereof they were divided into three congregations, one of which gathered for worship only on New Year and the Day of Atonement, the second owned a small synagogue, and the third met in an old dancing school. I preached on Saturday in the little synagogue, and on Sunday, which happened to be the ninth of *Av,* in the rented synagogue. I spoke quite unreservedly and without apology. I used plain language, and urged the union of the three congregations into one Reform congregation agreeable to the spirit of the age. This was done shortly after my departure. . . .

"Outside of Detroit, I had not, in the whole course of my journeyings, found one teacher, *ḥazan,* reader, or congregational official who had enjoyed even a common school education. I had come across not a single congregation that thought of reform. . . . The whole section of country through which I had travelled during these five or six weeks appeared to me, as far as Judaism was concerned, like a dead sea. There was no life, no effort, no becoming, no formation; and yet I was wrong. Every word that I spoke during that trip was a fruitful seed that took root and sought the light."

Success for Reform Judaism

Success came step by step for Isaac Mayer Wise. Many Jews began to accept the ideas of Reform Judaism for their synagogues, or temples. Wishing to give these congregations, as well as all the others in the country, a uniform ritual, or order of prayer, Rabbi Wise prepared a prayerbook which he called *Minhag America,* for he hoped it would become the standard prayerbook for all the American Jews.

In 1873, under Rabbi Wise's leadership, delegates of thirty-four congregations met in Cincinnati and formed the Union of American Hebrew Congregations. Two years later, the Hebrew Union College opened in Cincinnati to train American-born rabbis. Finally, Rabbi Wise organized the Central Conference of American Rabbis, an organization of Reform rabbis who were to meet each year to discuss the problems of their congregations and to make plans for the future.

Thus, as the movement of Reform Judaism reached its full strength in America, many congregations found union and leadership at last. And Isaac Mayer Wise became one of the great leaders and organizers of his people in the New World.

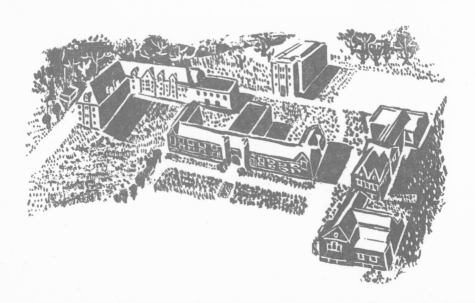

Sabato Morais

As Reform Judaism spread in the United States, Conservative Judaism too continued to gain ground. When Isaac Leeser resigned from Mikveh Israel, in 1850, and became *ḥazan* of another congregation, the man to take his place in Mikveh Israel was Sabato Morais, a fiery young rabbi who was born in Italy. In his native land, Sabato Morais and his family had allied themselves with the underground movement. Because of his sympathy with the revolutionaries, Sabato Morais was forced to leave Italy. He went to England, remaining there till he came to the United States to become rabbi of Mikveh Israel.

Sabato Morais was leader of the congregation during the Civil War, and the man who had been forced to leave his native land because of his love of freedom did not hesitate to express his political views when the southern states seceded from the Union. To Sabato Morais, secession meant the end of the one country that represented, to people everywhere, the land of freedom and opportunity. He therefore used his pulpit to denounce the southern states and to call for union and peace. When some of the members of the congregation opposed his use of the pulpit for expressing his own political opinions, the rabbi appealed to the entire congregation. The congregation supported Morais, giving him the right to speak on whatever subject he chose.

The Jewish Theological Seminary

The scholarly rabbi who had worked with all his energy for the union of the states turned this energy, when the time came, toward the establishment of a college for the training of rabbis. He had joined Leeser on the staff of Maimonides College. When the college closed, he worked with a group of men to found another school to take its place. Finally, in 1887, the Jewish Theological Seminary of America was opened in New York City, with Sabato Morais as its first president. Sabato Morais devoted the rest of his life to the Seminary, the academy which became the institution for training rabbis in the Conservative way of Judaism. Its full development, however, did not come till some years later, when Dr. Solomon Schechter came to America to be its head and to unite the Conservative congregations of the country.

But what of the Orthodox Jews in America, whose numbers were far greater than those of either the Reform or Conservative groups? The story of their organization came later, when a great new migration of Jews came to America from the lands of eastern Europe.

Things to Read

Lurie, Rose G., *The Great March,* "The Fight Is On," pp. 162-178.
Pessin, Deborah, *Giants On the Earth,* "I Took a Daring Leap," pp. 81-88.

Questions to Discuss

What goals did Isaac Mayer Wise and Isaac Leeser have in common? In what respects did they differ? To what extent were they able to work together despite their differences in outlook?

Things to Do

Visit the various synagogues and temples in your city. Discuss their similarities and their differences.

Pretend you are either an Isaac Leeser or an Isaac Mayer Wise of today. Write a few pages for your *Occident* or *Israelite,* using material about your own community.

Teachers Bibliography

Bentwich, Norman De Mattos, *Solomon Schechter, a biography,* Cambridge University Press, Cambridge, England, 1938.

Learsi, Rufus, *The Jews in America,* pp. 111-123.

Lebeson, Anita, *Pilgrim People,* pp. 296-375.

Wise, Isaac Mayer, *Reminiscences,* Leo Wise and Co., Cincinnati, 1901.

UNIT FOUR **THE NEW PIONEERS**

CHAPTER **1**

From the Land
of the Czars

The Rule of the Czars

While revolution swept through the lands of western Europe during the first half of the nineteenth century, creating constitutions, spreading the ideals of freedom, a great eastern land, larger than all the lands of the west combined, slumbered on in the medieval past. To Russia, change came slowly. The frozen steppes of this giant domain, the great primeval forests, the snowy reaches that ended only with the icy seas, seemed carved out of granite, unchanging as the sun and the stars. Only here and there, in the sprawling land of the Czars, were there faint stirrings among the people to show that they had felt a breath of the winds of freedom blowing from the west. Only here and there, in the few large cities of Russia, were the people awaking to the tyranny that oppressed them.

The Russian peasant, kept in bondage to his master from one generation to the next, toiled his life away like a beast of burden. In his dark, foul-smelling hut which he and his family shared with his horse, if he owned one, or with his cow, the peasant dreamed not of freedom—for he had never heard it spoken of—but of a pair of boots to cover his calloused foot or a warm cloak to shield him from the bitter winds.

For centuries, the Czars had not allowed Jews to settle in Russia. But in 1654 Russia seized the Ukraine from her neighbor, Poland, and since Jews had been living in the Ukraine, the Czars now had Jewish subjects. About a hundred years later Poland was partitioned by Austria, Russia and Prussia. In the section of land which was seized by Russia there lived almost a million Jews, the largest Jewish community in the world at that time. The Jews, whom the Czars wanted to keep out of Russia, were forbidden to live anywhere but in the section of land along Russia's western border. This section of land came to be called the Pale of Settlement.

Oppressed as was the general population of Russia, the Jews were even more oppressed. When a Czar, fearing the growing discontent of his people, threw them a few minor rights, he usually specified that all might enjoy these rights "except Jews."

In the Pale of Settlement

Isolated in the shabby villages of the Pale, the Jews saw little of the sprawling country in which they lived. They heard tales of the Czar, of the splendor of his palaces and the far reach of his reign, of large cities ablaze with lights where noblemen and their ladies rolled through the streets in carriages, of universities to which the rich sent their sons. But the Jews knew only the villages and towns of the Pale with their muddy lanes and shabby little houses. Here, like the Jews of the ghettoes in western Europe of a former age, they lived as their fathers had lived before them. Forbidden to own land, they were tailors, cobblers, tinsmiths, millers, carpenters, dealers in grain. Most of them were poor, working hard to make ends meet. Yet they were content, for there was no village so small that it did not have a synagogue, and a *heder* for their sons. Quietly

they lived on from one generation to the next, celebrating their festivals, observing their laws, dreaming of sending their sons to a famous *Yeshivah,* a rabbinical academy, or of marrying their daughters to *Yeshivah* students.

Pogroms and May Laws

Meanwhile, the movement for freedom in Russia slowly grew stronger. In 1861 Alexander II emancipated the serfs, and so came to be called the Emancipator Emperor. Young Russians, aware of what was happening in the western lands, demanded a constitution giving more rights to all the people. But even the Emancipator Emperor would not grant his people such a constitution. Czar Alexander II believed that the granting of rights would weaken the monarchy, and he replied to the demand for greater freedom by withdrawing many of the reforms he had introduced. Revolutionary students organized into secret societies, and one day in 1881, Alexander was assassinated. The day after the assassination Alexander III came to the throne.

Alexander III believed that his father had been too liberal with his subjects. He took, as his model, his grandfather, Nicholas I, who was known as the Iron Czar. Alexander III was aware of the poverty of millions of his subjects. He knew that resentment might turn into anger against the rulers and noblemen of Russia. And like many tyrants before him, Alexander decided to use the Jews as a scapegoat, diverting the resentment of the people away from himself and the noblemen and turning it against the Jews.

Rumors began to spread that the Jews were responsible for the death of Alexander II. It was the Jews, said the bearers of the rumors, who were responsible for the poverty of the peasants. Then pogroms, attacks against the Jews, were organized. Mobs broke into the villages, plundering and killing. From the south of Russia the pogroms spread northward, leaving death and ruin in their wake.

From America, England, France, from all parts of the civilized world came a storm of protests against the attacks on the Jews. Feeling he must do something to stop the outcries, Alexander had the pogroms stopped. But the Czar was not finished with persecut-

ing his Jewish subjects. For it was not the criminals who were punished, but the victims. In May, 1882, came the May Laws. These laws forced the Jews out of the villages in which they and their fathers had lived, into the larger towns of the Pale of Settlement. In the larger towns, already crowded with cobblers, tailors, storekeepers who could barely make a living, there was no work for them to do, no homes for them to live in. Suddenly, hundreds of thousands of Jews found themselves uprooted, facing starvation. In their desperation, many of them turned to America, the new Land of Promise.

The New Migration

They scraped together whatever money they could. They sold their feather beds, their family heirlooms, the few scraps of furniture they possessed. They fled west across Europe, by wagon, by train, on foot, through forests and towns. When they came to the harbor cities they bought third class tickets to bring them to America. Some of them, without money, were taken under the wing of special Jewish committees that had been set up to help them reach America. Many of them went hungry on the ships. Unwilling to eat food that was not *kosher,* they lived on the herring and bread they had brought with them. But they had a dream to keep them alive, the dream of America.

They came in 1881, the year of pogroms. They were cobblers, tailors, storekeepers, goldsmiths, tinsmiths, millers, who came. They came again in a mighty wave in 1882, the year of the May Laws, and in the years that followed. In 1905 large numbers of Russians rose in revolt against the Czar. The revolt was crushed, and hundreds of thousands more came to America, both Jews and Christians. This time there were also Jewish revolutionaries fleeing the vengeance of the Czar. To keep the people from rising against the monarchy because of starvation, pogroms were organized again in

1905, and again thousands of Jews fled across Europe, along the highway to the Golden Land.

Between 1881 and 1924 more than two million Jews came to America from eastern Europe, some from Romania, Galicia, Hungary, but most of them from Russia. After 1924, when Congress passed new laws limiting the number of immigrants permitted to enter the country, the immigration from eastern Europe was reduced to a trickle.

"The New Colossus"

At about the time when the pogroms began in Russia, there lived a young woman in the city of New York, Emma Lazarus, who was a descendant of Spanish Jews. Emma Lazarus liked to write poetry on classical themes. The young poet was far removed from the concerns and problems of her own people, till one day she visited some Jewish immigrants, women and children, waiting to be admitted to New York. Then, forgotten were the classical themes she had always loved, the gods and goddesses of ancient Greece. From the moment she saw her own people, the victims of tyranny, Emma Lazarus began to write poems of power and beauty as she had never written before.

In 1883 she wrote a sonnet, "The New Colossus." Twenty years later, in 1903, the sonnet was inscribed on a tablet and placed in the pedestal of the Statue of Liberty, symbol of America, the land of liberty.

Not like the brazen giant of Greek fame,
With conquering limbs astride from land to land;
Here at our sea-washed sunset gates shall stand
A mighty woman with a torch, whose flame
Is the imprisoned lightning, and her name
Mother of Exiles. From her beacon hand
Glows world-wide welcome; her mild eyes command
The air-bridged harbor that twin cities frame.

"Keep, ancient lands, your storied pomp!" cries she
With silent lips. "Give me your tired, your poor,
Your huddled masses yearning to breathe free,
The wretched refuse of your teeming shore,
Send these, the homeless, tempest-tost to me.
I lift my lamp beside the golden door!"

Things to Read

Leonard, Oscar, *Americans All,* "The Lamp Beside the Golden Door,"
    pp. 138-144.
Lurie, Rose G., *The Great March,* "Of Thee I Sing," pp. 162-178.
Pessin, Deborah, *Giants on the Earth,* "Emma Lazarus Comes Home
    Again," pp. 9-16.

Questions to Discuss

Why were the Czars successful in their scheme to use the Jews as scape-
goats?
Discuss Emma Lazarus' sonnet, "The New Colossus."

Things to Do

Send for one or both of the following films: "Immigration," distributed
    by Encyclopaedia Britannica Films; "Who Are the People of Amer-
    ica?" distributed by Ideal Pictures, Inc., 233 West 42nd St., New
    York 36, N. Y.
Find out from your parents and grandparents where they came from,
    what their background was like, why they came to America, the
    story of their first years in America. Use this material for your project,
    "Our Jewish Community."
Arrange an exhibit of objects, pictures, etc., which your relatives brought
    with them from the Old World.

Teachers Bibliography

Handlin, Oscar, *Adventure in Freedom,* pp. 80-108.
Learsi, Rufus, *The Jews in America,* pp. 124-147.

CHAPTER 2

Creating
a Better Life

Return to the Soil

In the early days of their history, when they were a nation in Palestine, the Jews had been an agricultural people. But the agricultural people, through the long centuries of exile, had been turned into an urban people. They had been denied the right to own land, shut into ghettoes and into the villages of the Pale of Settlement. Living in their close, narrow quarters, many Jews dreamed of owning land of their own and of living the free, open life of the farmer. Under Alexander I, Jews were encouraged to engage in agriculture, for the Czar wanted to populate Siberia. But very few Jews took advantage of the Czar's offer of land. They did not want to be uprooted from their own communities. In their little villages, they had, at least, their synagogues, their schools, their shops where they eked out a living. Who could tell, they thought, what might happen in distant Siberia. Not trusting the Czar, fearing the iron fist within the velvet glove, they remained in their own little villages.

Then came a movement from within, idealizing the life of the farmer. Many of their own writers, hoping that a new era of emancipation was dawning for the Jews, encouraged them to leave their dark little shops and turn to the soil. Still the Jews of the Pale remained in their villages, fearful of what the future might bring. And as it turned out, they were right in mistrusting the Czar. When the Russian government was no longer interested in encouraging the development of unsettled land, its attitude changed. Instead of encouraging the Jews to become farmers, it did all it could to hamper the movement to return to the soil.

But the movement did not die. Instead, it gained more and more followers. Eventually, two groups came into being, both with the aim of returning to an agricultural life. One group, BILU, took its name from the first letters of the Hebrew words of the prophet Isaiah, "House of Jacob, come, let us go up!" The plan of the BILU group was to return to the neglected land of their ancestors and to make it once more the fertile homeland it once had been. Members of the second group, *Am Olam,* "The Eternal People," joined the migration to America, hoping that somewhere in the Land of the Free they would be able to build a life of dignity close to the soil, showing the way for others of their people to follow. But because of their inexperience with working on the soil, their farm settlements failed, and gradually they drifted into the cities.

As Jewish refugees from eastern Europe kept pouring into the harbor cities, earlier settlers tried to help the newcomers. They founded organizations like the Hebrew Immigrant Aid Society, or HIAS, to help the immigrants find homes and work and to direct some of the flow to the less populated sections of the country. Baron de Hirsch, a rich German Jew who had settled in France, contributed millions of francs to establish farm settlements, first in Argentina, then in the United States. But the settlements, except for a few like the one in Woodbine, New Jersey, failed for lack of sufficient experience and guidance. In time, the Jewish Agricultural Society took over the task of helping Jewish farmers with funds, guidance and machinery. The work went on from year to year, and Jewish farms began to flourish. After the second World War, when thousands of new refugees came to America, the Jewish farm population increased, and by the middle of the twentieth century more than a hundred thousand Jews in America had returned to the agricultural life of their forefathers.

Living in the Cities

But the vast majority of Jews who came from eastern Europe remained in the industrial cities. They settled in Boston, Rochester, Baltimore. Some went to Philadelphia, some to Chicago, which had developed into a large, industrial center. Hundreds of thousands remained in the city of New York, close to their relatives and friends who had migrated before them. Because they were poor, they crowded into the older neighborhoods where rent was cheap, where their kinsmen had already settled, where they were sure to find synagogues, *kosher* butcher shops, schools for their children. Permitted now to live wherever they pleased, they chose to live close to each other, thus creating their own ghettoes.

As Jewish immigrants came streaming to the New World, the Jews of the lower East Side of New York City became the largest

Jewish community in the United States. The Irish, earlier immigrants than the east European Jews, had lived here before them, but when their conditions improved they moved to less congested neighborhoods and better houses. As the dark, dilapidated tenement flats of the lower East Side were vacated, Jewish immigrants moved in, happy to be with their own people.

The small flats of the lower East Side always had more people in them than they were meant to have. Only the "front room," often called the "parlor," had light from the street or from the rear courtyard. The other rooms had windows opening onto dark, narrow shafts, and in some flats, gaslight flickered all day in hot, airless kitchens. The "parlor" seldom served its original purpose, a room for entertaining guests. Often it became a bedroom. Folding beds came down at night for people to sleep on, usually for new arrivals from Russia who had no other place to go. If there was not enough space in the bedrooms and parlor for one's relatives or friends coming to America, there was always the kitchen where they could sleep till they found work and moved into a flat of their own. And often a family took in a boarder to help pay the rent.

Synagogues sprang up like mushrooms overnight, in cellars, stores, lofts. Men hailing from the same town prayed in the same synagogue, using the identical intonation and ritual. The immigrant from the lands of eastern Europe found no *ḥeder* in America which every Jewish boy was expected to attend. Instead, he found the public school, ready to teach his children English, history, arithmetic. This was a new experience for the Jewish immigrant. In Russia the Jews had generally been barred from the secular schools. In America they were required by law to send their children to school. The Jewish immigrant, however, did not require the law to ensure his sending his children to school. In Russia, he had resisted secular education for his children when it was offered him by the Czar, for he feared that the Czar's real purpose was to wean his children away from Judaism. In America, the immigrant had no

such fear. A man getting off the boat on Monday would often dash off to register his children in school on Tuesday.

But aside from the public school, the immigrant also wanted his *ḥeder,* so that his children would not forget the ways of their fathers. So he created a new type of *ḥeder,* which boys attended after public school. Sometimes *ḥeder* was in the home of the *rebbe,* or in someone's basement. Sometimes the *rebbe* went from house to house to teach the boys to read and recite their prayers. Like the synagogues, the *ḥeder* multiplied into hundreds, though the *rebbe* was not always a learned man. Often a man became a *rebbe* because he could find no other work to do.

The teeming streets of the lower East Side, like those in other industrial cities where Jews settled in large numbers, were never quiet, never deserted. Pushcarts lined the streets, and a housewife was able to get a good deal of what she needed for her home from the pushcart peddlers—apples, oranges, bananas, melons, tomatoes, cucumbers, potatoes, cabbage. Meat, of course, was bought from the *kosher* butcher shop, and milk, butter and eggs were bought at the little grocery store. The pushcart peddlers also sold handkerchiefs, linens, underwear, ribbon, bits of lace, safety pins, needles, scissors, knives, remnants of cloth that could be made up into dresses, aprons or curtains. Housewives went from pushcart to

pushcart looking for bargains, comparing prices, trying to save a penny or two on each item they bought so that they could make ends meet. Sometimes their bargains were second-hand goods or over-ripe fruit and vegetables. But the housewives of the lower East Side did not have enough money to insist on quality. They were satisfied if they could keep their families clothed and fed.

Rise of the Machine

Until far into the nineteenth century, most of the clothes the American people wore were made by hand. When a man who could afford to have good clothes needed a suit, his tailor made it for him. Abraham Lincoln, in 1843, needed a new suit of clothes. His wife Mary went to the Irwin General Store, where the Lincolns traded, and bought thirty dollars' worth of black material for her husband's suit. Abraham Lincoln was fitted by his tailor, and when the suit was finished the future President paid his tailor nine dollars for his work. Thirty-nine dollars was a large sum of money to pay for a suit in 1843, but Abe was doing well as a lawyer and he could afford to pay for expensive clothes. Most men in Lincoln's day had their suits made by their wives, and only a small percentage bought cheap, ready-made clothes.

When Mary Lincoln wanted some dresses or a cloak, she shopped for silks and taffetas and muslins. Then she called her seamstress, and for days on end the seamstress came to the Lincoln home where she cut, measured, snipped, basted, stitched. Poorer women sewed their own clothes as well as the clothes their children wore. It was easy to tell at a glance, as one walked down the street, which women had had an experienced seamstress make their clothes and which women had made their own clothes. The dress the poor woman wore was a bad copy of the dress the seamstress had made.

As the century progressed, machines were developed and more and more suits and dresses and cloaks were turned out in clothing factories. Although there were clothing factories in other industrial cities like Chicago, Boston, Rochester, most of them, many of them owned by German Jews, were in New York City, not far from the lower East Side. With the arrival of the immigrants from eastern Europe, the factory owners found that they suddenly had thousands of unskilled workers eager for work. It did not take much skill to operate a machine, and a lesson or two was all that was necessary to turn an unemployed immigrant into a wage-earner.

And so the clothing industry boomed in New York City. Factories worked to full capacity. New factories went up. Suits, cloaks and dresses were shipped to all parts of the United States. Designers developed their skill, paying more attention to the cut of a garment and to the details, so that it became difficult to tell the difference between a custom-made and a ready-made garment. The people in the United States became the best dressed people in the world. Orders came to the factories from all parts of the country as more and more immigrants were hired to turn out clothes for the American people.

Meeting the Boat

In the meantime, ships kept coming to Castle Garden, at the gateway to New York City, leaving new groups of immigrants from eastern Europe. Families were met by officials of HIAS who helped them get settled, find homes, work, relatives. Often the immigrants were met by factory owners who spoke Yiddish, the language of the east European Jews. Hearing the familiar tongue made the immigrant feel more at home, as though he already had friends in the New World.

"Do you want work?" a manufacturer would ask the head of a family.

"Work? Of course I want work."

"Then come with me."

Relatives were often at hand, proudly wearing their American clothes.

"Ah, Solomon, now you are here."

"You have changed, Berel. One would hardly recognize you in your American clothes. And you have taken off your beard."

"One changes in America. And in the old country, in the home town, is there anyone left?"

"Eliezer and his family, Moshe and his family. . . . But they are planning to come to America."

"Well, come, I will show you everything."

"Where are you taking me? Such a wilderness! So many people!"

"Naturally, you will stay with me. We will put up beds in the front room."

"And where will I work? What will I do?"

"You will find work in my shop. You will sew dresses."

"Sew dresses! How can I sew dresses?"

"It is easy. I will show you how."

Sweatshops

With every ship coming to Castle Garden, more immigrants crowded into the lower East Side, where they could be close to their friends. Their friends introduced them to the New World, taking them to their shops and factories and synagogues. From time to time a family that had made good moved away from the lower East Side. They moved uptown or out to Brooklyn. But the dark rooms they vacated were quickly snatched up by new immigrants.

In time, clothing manufacturers found that it was cheaper to parcel out their work to contractors, instead of crowding their factories with machines and workmen. Many of them began to employ only cutters who, following a pattern, cut the material that was to be sewn up into garments. Then they made bundles of the cut material. The contractors came for the bundles, and since there were many contractors competing for them, the manufacturer gave his bundles to those who offered to get the work done for the least amount of money. The contractors took the bundles to their dark, airless flats on the lower East Side. These flats were the shops, which came to be called "sweatshops," where thousands of Jewish immigrants sewed the garments that went out to the American people.

In the kitchen of the sweatshop the pressers worked, for they needed to heat their irons at the stove. The machine workers, basters, finishers, occupied the rest of the flat. Sometimes the flat was so crowded that there was no room to walk about. Machines were often put out in the dark hallways, on the fire escapes, anywhere where there was room for a machine. Mingling with the workers was the contractor's family, his wife cooking in the kitchen, his children wandering in and out.

Men and women worked at their machines from early morning till late in the evening, often as much as fourteen hours a day. A man's wages usually came to six or eight dollars a week, a woman's to less, often as little as three. Since the contractor, eager to get the work, had offered to have the garments sewn for less than his competitor, and since he too had to make a living, he paid his workmen as little as possible. A worker was not paid weekly wages. He was paid by the "piece," which meant that he was paid for each garment he finished. To sew more garments, he would have to work longer hours. At four o'clock in the morning, the streets of the lower East Side would already be filled with men and women on their way to work. Sometimes, to save the time wasted in coming and going, workers would sleep on the floors of the sweatshops, row upon row, their heads cushioned on bundles. A worker could not threaten to leave if he did not receive higher wages, for there were always plenty of other immigrants ready to take his place. Workers often had to buy their own sewing machines, and when the electric machine became popular, they paid for the electric current as well.

So the immigrant was bound to his sweatshop, dreaming, perhaps, of a day when he himself would be a contractor, or even a manu- facturer, a "boss." For had not many of the manufacturers them- selves started as humble workmen? The weeks, months and years went by, and the dreams remained only dreams. And the machine- worker, brooding over his lot, wondered why they had called Amer- ica the Golden Land. All he knew was hard toil and privation, and even worse, the fear that some day there might be no work. Through illness and hunger, men and women sat at their machines, sewing suits, cloaks, dresses, shirt-waists. Snow fell in the streets. Spring followed winter. But it did not matter to the machine-worker bent over his work in the dark, unsanitary flat where gaslight flickered throughout the days and nights and seasons. Many workers developed tuberculosis in the sweatshops. Their faces pale and drawn, their aching bodies racked with coughs, they did not dare leave their work for fear of starvation.

Workers would often take bundles home to their own flats. By working at home, a man could have his whole family to help him. When the meager evening meal was over and the table cleared, the bundle was opened, and husband, wife and children all bent over their work, stitching away till the early hours of morning. Throughout the night, the hum of the sewing machine could be heard on the streets of the lower East Side.

The Slack Season

Much as the worker hated the sweatshops, he dreaded the time, each year, when there was little or no work. These months, called the slack season, came periodically and meant actual hunger for thousands of families. Because of his low wages, the worker had been able to save very little, or nothing at all, to help tide him over the slack season. When the lean months came, hunger stared him in the face. He borrowed wherever he could. His wife, when she had any, cooked her potatoes with their skins on so that none of the potato would be wasted. He tried to get credit at the grocery, but the grocer too had to earn a living. The slack season was the plague of the lower East Side, threatening not only the workers, but the neighborhood dealers, the pharmacist at the drug store, the visiting doctor, the butcher, the baker, the fish peddler. If people had no money, they could not pay for services or merchandise. Even the teachers in the public schools were affected by the slack season. When they could no longer bear to see the hungry, pale little faces, they would slip the hungriest looking of the children a few coins to buy food.

Forming Unions

For a long time, conditions in America had been changing. The early pioneer America, where each man could carve out his own future, had become a nation of farmers, manufacturers, factory workers, retail dealers, laborers, all depending on one another for the money they earned. The great grandson of the pioneer who had hacked trees out of the forest to build his home worked in a factory or a mill, turning out the goods America needed. As immigrants came to the United States from Ireland, Germany, England, Russia, Italy, the army of factory workers grew larger and larger. Working conditions were poor everywhere, with long hours, unsanitary conditions and low wages. Then men began to realize that they could not ask for higher wages or improve their working conditions alone. They must do it together, as a group, or union. So unions began to be formed, now in one industry and now in another. The unions grew stronger, and gradually the working day was shortened, wages were increased, working conditions were improved.

Men and women on the lower East Side began to hear about unions, how people were able to improve their conditions if they acted as a group instead of individually. Some of the workers in the sweatshops had been students of the Talmud in the Old Country. They had had dreams of coming to America and entering the professions. Instead, unable to afford to go to school, they found themselves in sweatshops, barely earning a living. They entered American socialist movements which they hoped would create a better world for the poor and oppressed. They talked to the men and women in the sweatshops about the need for setting up unions. And slowly unions began to form, and now and then a strike was called. At the turn of the century, when the revolution in Russia failed,

Jews who had been in the revolutionary movement and had fled to America led the workers in the needle trades—the dress and cloak makers, the fur workers, the cap and hat makers—in the building of unions.

The unions remained weak for a long time. When the workers of a shop went out on strike they usually went out alone, without the help of other shops. It was not difficult to break such a strike, and the employers often turned the strike into a lockout, which meant that the workers were not permitted to return to work in the shop.

Success came step by step. Failure of a strike meant harder work for the union officials in organizing more workers, so that the next strike would be more effective. Workers learned that the small groups must unite into large ones. Again and again they struck for better conditions, and with each successful strike the unions grew stronger. Strikes meant suffering to the workers, for they received no wages during the time they did not work and they had to depend on the limited union funds to keep them going till they could earn money again. But the example of other unions and the hope of improving their conditions goaded them on to build their unions stronger.

Finally, in 1900, the workers in the ladies' garments industry united in the International Ladies Garment Workers Union. In November, 1909, twenty thousand young women in New York City who worked at women's blouses, most of them girls, struck for better working conditions. They sent their two thousand delegates to Cooper Union, where they heard speaker after speaker make long speeches on the wisdom of the strike and how to carry it through. Weary of the speeches, eager for action, a young girl rose to her feet and called for a general strike. "Do you mean it in good faith?" a leader demanded. "Will you take the old Jewish oath?" Two thousand hands were raised as the delegates in unison chanted an adaptation of the old Jewish oath, "If I turn traitor to the cause I now pledge, may the hand wither from the arm I now raise."

The strike began. Never before had so many workers of the lower East Side left their shops together. "The Uprising of the Twenty Thousand," as it was called, caused wild excitement among the workers of the needle trades. And when it was won, its success encouraged others to strike for better conditions in their own branches of the industry.

About five months later came the "Great Revolt," planned for many weeks by its leaders. This time sixty thousand workers of the International Ladies Garment Workers Union left their shops. On July 7, 1910, the day the strike was called, they were instructed to leave their shops at two o'clock and proceed to certain halls for meetings. Members of the strike committee and members of the press went to the cloak district to see if the workers would obey the summons. Two o'clock came, and there was no worker to be seen on the streets. "Well," a newspaper editor remarked to the strike committee, "where are your strikers?"

At that moment they came. "Hardly had he spoken," said one of the strike leaders later, "than we saw a sea of people surging from all the side streets toward Fifth Avenue. . . . By half-past two, all the streets, from Thirty-eighth Street down and from the East River towards the west, were jammed with thousands of workers. . . . Many of our most devoted members cried for joy at the idea that their life-long labors had at last been crowned with success. In my mind I could only picture to myself such a scene taking place when the Jews were led out of Egypt."

The sixty thousand workers struck for higher wages, better working conditions and a closed shop, which meant that only union members could be hired by an employer. The employers refused to grant the demands, and the strike dragged on through July, then

through August. Newspapers carried the story of the Great Revolt, and many thousands of Americans learned for the first time about sweatshop conditions. Prominent Americans tried to arbitrate between strikers and employers. Louis Dembitz Brandeis, a Boston lawyer who was to become a Justice of the Supreme Court and who was a descendant of a Jewish family that had migrated to America from Bohemia, was one of the men who tried to help the strikers and employers reach an agreement. He suggested the "preferential shop," which meant that if an employer had a choice between hiring a union and a non-union man, he was to give preference to the union man.

In September, the Great Revolt ended. Arrangements were made for workers and employers to get together over disagreements, so that strikes might be avoided in the future if possible. Some of the manufacturers had had no notion of the unbearable conditions in

their factories, and they were relieved to have the opportunity to improve conditions in the industry. A permanent committee was set up to deal with grievances, and a Board of Arbitration was to handle more important issues. A Joint Board of Sanitary Control was set up to do away with unsanitary conditions in the factories. The sweatshops lingered on for some time, since they could not be wiped out overnight, but wages went up, conditions were improved, and in time the sweatshops became a thing of the past.

At about the same time that the International Ladies Garment Workers Union held its Great Revolt, another strike broke out in Chicago among the workers in the men's clothing industry. The strike was not planned in advance, as was that of the International Ladies Garment Workers Union. Workers of one shop left their machines and tools. Wives of the strikers spread news of the strike to women they met in the streets or in the stores of their neighborhood. As men in non-striking shops heard the news, they too left their work. In three weeks forty thousand people were out on strike. The strike dragged on into the winter, bringing great hardship to the workers. Storekeepers, newspapers, clubs, churches, individuals, all helped with contributions. The gas company agreed to go on supplying gas in the homes of strikers who could not pay their bills. Finally an arbitration committee representing both employers and employees was set up. The Amalgamated Clothing Workers Union had won its first important victory. Like the International Ladies Garment Workers Union, it had gone through many years of trial and error before it emerged strong enough to create decent living standards for its workers.

Pioneering in Industry

The needle trades unions did more than just raise the standard of living for its workers. They pioneered in establishing better relations between employers and employees, setting up committees and boards to bring the two sides together to discuss their differences. They pioneered in bringing their members social, educational and health service. When a worker did not have to worry continually about how to make ends meet, his mind was free to turn to other matters—to studies and recreation. The International Ladies Garment Workers Union established classes for its members and arranged lectures, concerts, dances, boatrides, picnics. It set up a vacation resort, and a health clinic which offered its members low cost medical and dental care. The Amalgamated established its own banks in Chicago and New York, and large cooperative housing projects which provided families with apartments for far less than they had paid for their unsanitary tenement flats.

Thinking of the dreaded slack seasons when the workers could earn no money, the unions pioneered in unemployment insurance long before the federal government made it part of its national program. Both employees and employers contributed each week to the unemployment fund, the workers a small percentage of their weekly wages and the employers a small percentage of the payroll. When the slack season came, the unemployed received a percentage of their regular salaries. Thus was eliminated the fear of hunger which had hung over the workers like a threatening cloud even during the busy seasons.

Labor Leaders

Jews had entered many industries besides the needle trades. They were glaziers, bricklayers, carpenters, watchmakers, cigarmakers, painters. With their fellow Americans, they built unions in whichever industry they had entered to make a living. Sometimes they were leaders in the building of unions.

One of the most important of America's labor leaders was Samuel Gompers, a Jewish immigrant who came to America from England when he was a boy of ten and began work as a cigar-maker. Gompers spent almost all his life organizing workers, first in his own trade, then in others. He became one of the founders of the powerful American Federation of Labor and served as its president for almost forty years, till his death in 1924.

Like Samuel Gompers, the leaders in the needle trades unions began in the ranks. David Dubinsky, who was born in Russia, went to *heder* and was a student of the Talmud. Early in his youth, Dubinsky was drawn into the revolutionary movement, and when his activities were discovered by the police he was thrown into prison. Released from prison, he came to America, to the city of New York, where he became a cutter in a clothing factory. When the factory and sweatshop workers began to form their unions, Dubinsky became one of their leaders, finally reaching the post of president of the International Ladies Garment Workers Union. This post Dubinsky held for many years, leading the members of the union to greater and greater gains.

Sidney Hillman too was born in eastern Europe, in Lithuania. His parents expected their son to be a rabbi, and for several years he attended a *Yeshivah,* a rabbinical academy. When the lad was eighteen years old he became active in the revolutionary movement, was imprisoned, and finally released. Coming to America, he found his way to Chicago, where he worked in a clothing factory for six dollars a week.

Hillman led the famous strike of 1910, when forty thousand workers left their shops, and a few years later he became first president of the Amalgamated Clothing Workers Union of America, a position he held for the rest of his life.

In 1933, President Franklin Delano Roosevelt, planning the New Deal which he hoped would bring greater economic security to the American people, invited Sidney Hillman to be a member of the Labor Advisory Board of the National Recovery Act. In 1940, when war with Germany was drawing near and when it was important to keep the wheels of industry moving, the President appointed Hillman a member of his National Defense Advisory Commission. A short time later, the labor leader took over the work of director of the Labor Division of the Office of Production Management. For twenty-four years Hillman served his union, the Amalgamated, as well as the nation at large.

The pioneers from eastern Europe, like those who had come before them, hewed out a place for themselves in the New World. From their tenement flats and sweatshops and factories, out of their hunger and striving, they created a better life for themselves and for hundreds of thousands of their fellow Americans. And throughout their struggle for a livelihood, they thought of the future of their children. Often they deprived themselves, living on crusts, so that their children could have a college education and enjoy the full cultural life America offered.

Things to Read

Leonard, Oscar, *Americans All,* "He Championed Labor," pp. 163-172; "And Children Loved Her," pp. 180-186.

Questions to Discuss

How did the fact that the Jews had become an urban people in the countries of Europe affect their life in the New World?

Why was it natural for many German Jewish immigrants to become peddlers, and for many immigrants from eastern Europe to become factory workers?

Things to Do

If you live in a large, industrial city where Jews from eastern Europe
settled in large numbers, arrange to visit the neighborhood where
they went to live when they first came to America. Find out, if possible, what remains of the old days, which of their synagogues and
schools still exist, where many of them have moved. Find out what
new institutions and organizations they built as they became adjusted
to the New World. Use your material for your project, "Our Jewish
Community."

Write a letter for an immigrant in a large city to a relative or friend in
the old country. Tell him about life in America.

Teachers Bibliography

Antin, Mary, *The Promised Land,* Houghton Mifflin Co., Boston,
1912.

Bernheimer, Charles S., *The Russian Jew in the United States,* John
C. Winston Co., New York, 1905.

Davidson, Gabriel, *Our Jewish Farmers,* L. B. Fischer Publishing
Co., New York, 1943.

Learsi, Rufus, *The Jews in America,* pp. 148-167.

Reznikoff, Charles, *By the Waters of Manhattan,* Boni, New York,
1930.

Stolberg, Benjamin, *Tailor's Progress,* Doubleday Doran, Garden
City, 1944.

CHAPTER **3**

Organization of Jewish Community Life

Helping the Newcomers

By the time the Jews of eastern Europe, or the "Russian Jews," as they were often called, began to arrive in America, the German Jews had all but forgotten their own pioneering days. The hard-working immigrants from the Germanic lands had become prosperous merchants, factory owners, leaders in industry, politicians. Their children had attended the colleges and universities and had entered the professions. They had built synagogues, temples, hospitals, orphanages, homes for the aged, charitable organizations. They had established centers, like the Young Men's Hebrew Association, and had founded important lodges, like B'nai B'rith. Grown part of America, the habits and the suffering of the past forgotten, the German Jews felt at home with the world about them.

Then suddenly, wave upon wave, came the Russian Jews, frightened, shabby, trailing the shadows of poverty and persecution. To the German Jews they seemed spectres of themselves rising out of

201

a past they had taken pains to forget. For they too had come shabby and lonely to the New World. They too had been haunted by fear of hunger and of the customs of an unfamiliar way of life. Though the first reaction of many German Jews was dismay, and a horror of being associated with the shabby immigrants, they rallied to help them and to introduce them to American life.

The charitable organizations already existing were not enough to take care of the new masses of immigrants coming from the Old World. They set up new organizations, like HIAS, to help the immigrants crowding into the cities. Women's auxiliaries of synagogues and temples sewed clothes and prepared baskets of food for the newcomers. Night classes were organized in settlement houses and in Y.M.H.A.'s to teach the immigrants the language and customs of the country. In the city of Baltimore, the daughter of Rabbi Benjamin Szold, Henrietta, opened a night school in several rooms above a store. Weary from their day of work, men and women, young and old, came to Henrietta Szold's school and sat on long wooden

benches, learning to spell, to read, and to speak the English language. Soon other subjects were introduced—arithmetic, bookkeeping, sewing. As the number of students increased, Henrietta Szold hired several assistants. By 1898, when the Board of Education took over the night school, one of the first in the country, five thousand immigrants, Jews and Christians, had received instruction in Henrietta Szold's "Russian School."

Old Institutions on New Soil

Despite all the help they received, however, the Russian Jews found that for the most part, they must help themselves. The gap between the Russian and the German Jews was wide. Their speech, their customs, their background were different. The Russian Jews, most of them Orthodox, established their own synagogues, the kind they were accustomed to, where men and women were separated, where there was no organ music, where the rabbi's sermon was given in Yiddish.

The Russian Jews also set up their own type of school, the *heder*, where the *rebbe* taught his pupils to read their prayers and, sometimes, to translate passages of the Bible into Yiddish. As they had done in the old country, the east European Jews also established Talmud Torahs for the children of the poor who could not pay tuition.

But like most things brought from one country to another, the institutions of the Russian Jews underwent change. The *heder* could not flourish as it had in Russia, where it was the only school the child attended and where it was part of his life. In America the boy went to public school, and he did not want to be shut up in a dark room with a *rebbe* he considered old-fashioned and who spoke in a language he was quickly forgetting. Strangely enough, in America it was the Talmud Torah which turned out to be a better school than the *heder*.

Beginning as a little school which only boys attended, the Talmud Torah gradually developed. And as it developed, it began to appeal more and more to the parents of the children who attended *ḥeder*. In time, it ceased to be a charitable institution supported by people who would not send their own children to it. The little Talmud Torah became a large establishment, where young teachers replaced the *rebbe,* and where girls as well as boys were admitted. The teachers were able to teach their pupils more than just the reading of prayers. They taught Hebrew as a language, Bible, some history, Hebrew songs, current events. Realizing that it had become superior to the *ḥeder,* parents began to send their children to the Talmud Torah instead of to the *ḥeder.* For a long time the Talmud Torah remained the Jewish school of the Russian Jews.

As the Russian Jews grew more prosperous and secure, they began to move away from the "ghettoes" they had created. They too began to build large, handsome synagogues, as the Conservative and Reform Jews had done. Then both Talmud Torah and *ḥeder,* like the little synagogue in a loft above a store, also began to disappear. Special rooms were set aside in the new synagogues to serve as classrooms for the children, both boys and girls.

Yiddish

The Yiddish language, which had flourished in the east European lands for many centuries, became, in America, the cultural instrument for hundreds of thousands of Jews. Yiddish was the language of the street, the home, the shop, the factory, the synagogue. While children who went to public school might speak to their parents in English, their parents replied in Yiddish, with perhaps a sprinkling of English words.

To satisfy the hunger of the immigrants for information and knowledge, Yiddish newspapers, magazines and books were pub-

lished. The worker returning from work in the evening picked up his Yiddish newspaper at the newsstand. When he finished his dinner and his wife cleared the table, he put on his spectacles and spread out his newspaper. Then the great wide world opened before him. He read not only the news of the day, but stories by his favorite writers, instructions on how to vote, articles on the history of the United States, advice to the lovelorn, romances in serial form. He laughed as he read a humorous story by Sholom Aleichem, and he pondered over an article on the American Constitution. His newspaper drew him out of his own narrow orbit into the wide world beyond the streets he walked each day and the people he knew.

Like the newspaper, the Yiddish theatre opened wider horizons to the immigrant Jew. Though there were Yiddish theatres in other large cities, it was Second Avenue in New York City that became the center of the Yiddish stage. Going to the Yiddish theatre was a happy occasion, whether the play was a tragedy or a comedy. Sitting among his friends, the theatre-goer of the lower East Side saw dramas based on domestic life or on historical themes. The exploits of Judah Maccabee unfolded before his dazzled eyes, and the story of Bar Kokhba, the Golem, Shabbatai Zevi. He might never have heard of Shakespeare, but he was sure to see a translation of *King Lear* or *Hamlet*. Or he might have seen tragedies or comedies dealing with people in his own day.

For more than half a century the Yiddish theatre transported the peddler, the sweatshop worker and the storekeeper from their humdrum lives to a world of romance and fancy. But as happened with the *ḥeder,* the Yiddish theatre could not flourish indefinitely. Gradually it declined as the children of the east European Jews began to prefer the English theatre to the Yiddish one their parents had enjoyed.

Landsmanschaften

No sooner did the east European Jews come to America than they began to form little societies, *landsmanschaften,* consisting of those who came from the same hamlet or town or city. Thus there were hundreds of large and small *landsmanschaften* for Minsk, Pinsk, Dvinsk, Bialostok, Grodno, Lodz, Odessa, Kiev, Vilna, Volozhin, Telz, Warsaw, Zhitomir. . . . There was scarcely a town in Russia where Jews had lived that was not represented by a *landsmanschaft* in America. For distance lent charm to the old country, and people liked to gather with those they had known in childhood to muse about the past and to sigh for the by-gone days, however unhappy they had been. The *landsmanschaft* met for mutual-aid as well as for cultural and social reasons. Some of the smaller *landsmanschaften* did not last very long, but some grew stronger and larger, often banding together to collect money for Palestine and for their persecuted people in foreign lands.

Attempt at Unity

Hundreds of thousands of new arrivals to a country, remaining, for the most part, in the large cities, created new needs which could not be handled by the older institutions. Just as the small charity societies had given way to larger ones, the larger ones now found that their time too was passing. It was an organization called, in most cities, Federation, which came to take the place of the charitable organizations. Sometimes, for a short period, there would be two federations in one city, a "German" federation of charities, and a "Russian" federation of charities. But as the groups learned to work together, the two federations united into one which served the entire Jewish community of the city.

It was around the turn of the century, too, that people began to make efforts to bring some order into the chaos of Jewish life in the larger cities. One of these people was Judah L. Magnes, an American-born rabbi and scholar. Rabbi Magnes saw the hundreds of synagogues and temples, most of them going their own way, the hundreds of Jewish schools without a central agency to guide them, the many *landsmanschaften* and lodges often duplicating one another's work. Judah Magnes envisioned the chaos turning into order. He dreamed of seeing the Jews of America united into one body, as they had been united in the lands of eastern Europe in the *kahal*, developing a rich culture with a central authority which would speak for all the Jews of America.

In 1909, under the leadership of Dr. Magnes, representatives of various organizations met in New York City and set up a *kehillah*, a "community." The organizers of the *kehillah* hoped that other cities too would set up their *kehillot*, and that representatives of the *kehillot* would meet in a central agency. The New York *kehillah* began by establishing a court to handle religious disputes, a welfare board which was to handle social problems, and a Bureau of Jewish Education. But the New York *kehillah* did not succeed, for many people were not ready to accept its authority. The Bureau of Jewish Education, which was headed by Dr. Samson Benderly, continued, however, to be the central agency for many Jewish schools for a number of years. Other cities too, at this time, began to set up Bureaus of Jewish Education. The Bureau of Jewish Education of New York City gave way, in 1922, to the Jewish Education Association, and this organization eventually merged with the Jewish Education Committee of New York, the central organization of Jewish education for the entire Jewish community in New York City and its environs.

Though the *kehillah* organized by Dr. Magnes lived but a short time, the idea did not die. Dr. Mordecai M. Kaplan, a member of the staff of the Jewish Theological Seminary, began a movement called Reconstructionism. Judaism, he said, was not just a religion. It was a civilization of which religion was the central part. To live a creative and complete Jewish life, said Dr. Kaplan, the Jews must organize themselves into communities in which all the features of their civilization would be developed and all their organizations democratically represented. To further the idea of Reconstructionism, Dr. Kaplan founded a magazine, the *Reconstructionist,* and an organization, The Reconstructionist Foundation, which some rabbis, laymen and even synagogues joined without breaking away from their national synagogue organizations.

Growth of the Seminary

The mass movement of the Jews from the lands of eastern Europe also spurred the Jewish Theological Seminary on to greater efforts to satisfy the growing need for religious leaders. Looking for a presi-

dent who would be acceptable to the Jews of the eastern lands as well as to those coming from the western lands, the Seminary decided that the man was Solomon Schechter, a member of the faculty of Cambridge University.

Solomon Schechter, born in Romania, had his roots in the east. After receiving a thorough education in Jewish subjects in his native land, he went to Vienna, where he absorbed the culture of the western world. Schechter's fame as a scholar earned him an invitation to come to Cambridge. It was here that still greater fame came to the scholar. For Schechter discovered in a *genizah* (a storeroom for old books) in a synagogue in Cairo, many valuable old Hebrew manuscripts and books. Among these was the Hebrew manuscript of *Ecclesiasticus,* or Book of Ben Sirah, a manuscript which had been the object of search by scholars for many years.

In 1902, invited by the Seminary to be its president, Solomon Schechter left Cambridge for America. When Schechter came to the Jewish Theological Seminary, he asked a number of young scholars to join the staff—Louis Ginzberg, Alexander Marx, Israel Friedlander, Israel Davidson, Mordecai Kaplan. It was then that the Seminary gained a reputation for scholarship, but so great was Dr. Schechter's personal influence that the school was often referred to as the Schechter Seminary.

In 1913, Dr. Schechter founded the United Synagogue of America, an organization of Conservative congregations, and several years later, graduates of the Seminary, together with other Conservative rabbis, founded the Rabbinical Assembly of America.

Dr. Schechter also wanted to reach the children in the Jewish schools through teachers educated in America, teachers who had a background similar to that of their pupils. To educate such teachers, he founded the Teachers Institute, appointing Mordecai M. Kaplan as its dean. In time there was a group of young men and women, educated in America, ready to take the place of the *rebbe*, the teacher from the Old World who was gradually disappearing from the American scene.

The schools attached to the Conservative synagogues, meanwhile, had been developing into congregational schools, where the children usually met for instruction three days a week, while the schools attached to the Reform temples were generally Sunday schools, where the chief studies were Bible stories, Jewish history and religion. As the congregational schools gained greater popularity, the curriculum was enriched with more studies. In addition to Hebrew, the prayers and the Bible, the pupils were taught Jewish history, current events, Hebrew songs, and the religious observances of their people. In some schools, art work and dramatics became part of the program, and in time, all the congregational schools introduced Sabbath services for the children.

Organization of East European Jews

In the meantime, the east European Jews were developing stronger religious and educational institutions. Organization, however, did not come for a long time, though now and then congregations tried to get together under a central authority. This happened once in 1888, when fifteen leading Orthodox congregations in New York invited Rabbi Jacob Joseph of Vilna to come to America to be their Chief Rabbi. It was a great day for the lower East Side when their Chief Rabbi arrived. Rabbi Jacob Joseph's ship docked in Hoboken, New Jersey, on a Sabbath morning, and since the rabbi would not debark on the Sabbath, he spent the day aboard ship. On the other side of the river thousands of people waited impatiently for sundown, and when evening services were over, delegates of the congregations took the ferry to Hoboken and escorted the sage from Vilna to the home they had rented for him on the lower East Side. By now the crowds milling about were so

large that the police had to be called out. Many people wept for joy
at sight of the dignified, learned rabbi who had come from the Old
World to be their spiritual leader.

Organization on a large scale, however, did not come till 1902,
when hundreds of rabbis united in the Union of Orthodox Rabbis
of the United States and Canada. Later, other unions of Orthodox
rabbis were formed. One of the most important was the Rabbinical
Council of America, an organization of Orthodox rabbis educated
in America.

The *Yeshivah* too was an institution developed by the east European Jews. In Russia the *Yeshivah* had been a rabbinical academy.
In America it became a school where the child received both a Jewish and a secular education. The famous Yeshivah University had
its beginning back in 1897, when a school was organized on the
lower East Side and named for a great sage, the Isaac Elḥanan
Yeshivah. But difficulties soon arose in the school. The students

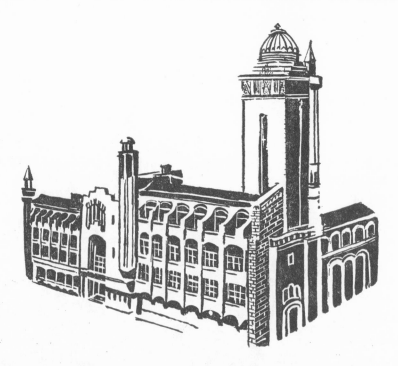

were not content to study Hebrew subjects simply for the sake of study. They wanted their studies to lead to the rabbinate, and they wanted, in addition, to learn the secular subjects of the high schools and colleges.

So Yeshivah, as the Isaac Elḥanan Yeshivah came to be called, was forced to make adjustments to suit the needs of their students in the New World. Students were permitted to register in high schools and colleges until the time when Yeshivah was prepared to offer secular subjects in its own classrooms. When Dr. Bernard Revel was called to be its director and guide, Yeshivah began to expand, adding more departments, a high school and a Teachers Institute. Yeshivah went on growing from year to year, becoming a college as well as a rabbinical seminary. Finally, in 1945, it became a university, and in 1955 it added a medical school called the Albert Einstein Medical School and Center in honor of the famous Jewish scientist.

Working Together

Orthodox Jewry, Conservative Jewry, Reform Jewry, each had built its institutions in the New World. But the lines between the three groups were not rigid. Children of Orthodox parents sometimes joined a Reform temple or a Conservative synagogue. Children of Reform or Conservative parents often drifted to one of the other groups.

Nor did the three groups always work alone. When the need arose, they united their efforts to protect their rights. When their people abroad needed help, they built new organizations together so that their work would be more effective. The Zionist organizations drew their greatest support at first from the east European Jews. But in time Jews from all groups worked together for the rebuilding of Israel's ancient homeland. And so it was with other organizations which united all the Jews of America for reaching a common goal. In 1926, the three groups organized the Synagogue Council of America, so that the national bodies of synagogues and rabbis could cooperate in religious matters which concerned all the Jews of the country.

From their timid beginnings in September 1654, when twenty-three refugees landed in New Amsterdam, the Jews of America had grown into a strong community. Bit by bit, sometimes against great odds, they had established themselves economically. And often, as difficult as the struggle to make a living was the struggle to build their own way of life. But they succeeded, after many trials and errors, in developing the institutions that best suited their needs. Because the Jews came from every part of the world, their background, their language, even their way of worship, were not always the same. That is why, in adjusting themselves to American life, they built different kinds of synagogues, schools, lodges, philanthropies. Coming from lands of oppression, they learned, in America, to cherish and defend the freedom they had helped to build. And so, when they encountered prejudice or slander, they set up defense organizations like the Anti-Defamation League of B'nai Brith, like the American Jewish Committee and the American Jewish Congress, to speak and act for them. Through these organizations, they defended not only themselves, not only their people in other lands, but the American principles of democracy. In the variety of cultures and customs which live equally side by side in the New World, the Jews built a way of life which was true to themselves as Jews and true to the spirit of America.

Things to Read

Alofsin, Dorothy, *America's Triumph,* "The Voice in Her Heart," pp. 109-135.

Edidin, Ben M., *Jewish Community Life in America,* Hebrew Publishing Co., New York, 1947.

Lurie, Rose G., *The Great March,* "The Hidden Treasure," pp. 217-228.

Pessin, Deborah, *Giants on the Earth,* "Rescued," pp. 89-100.

Questions to Discuss

Compare the life of the east European Jews in the Old World with their life in America. Discuss their opportunities, their economic conditions, their cultural and religious institutions.

What features of their life in Europe did the Russian Jews retain? How did they change in America?

Why didn't the *Kehillah* organized by Judah Magnes succeed? Do you think it could be made to work now? How?

Things to Do

If there are any rabbinical seminaries, Jewish teachers institutes or colleges in your city, arrange to visit them to learn something about their origins and the work they do.

Send to your federation and relief agencies for material describing their work.

Write to Educational Services, 1730 I Street, N.W., Washington, D. C., for the records "The Jews," in the series, "Immigrants All—Americans All."

Write to the Council of Jewish Federations and Welfare Funds, 165 West 46 St., N.Y. 19, N. Y., for their filmstrip, "Wherever Help Is Needed."

Write to the Los Angeles Jewish Community Council, 590 N. Vermont Ave., Los Angeles 4, California, for their film, "The Key to '53," and to the Associated Jewish Charities of Baltimore, 319 W. Monument Street, Baltimore 1, Maryland, for the film, "Behind the Pledge."

Bring your map of migrations, your mural, and your project, "Our Jewish Community," up to date.

Teachers Bibliography

Handlin, Oscar, *Adventure in Freedom,* pp. 109-174; pp. 211-261.
Learsi, Rufus, *The Jews in America,* pp. 183-216.

NEW
RESPONSIBILITIES

CHAPTER **1**

Help Overseas

The Damascus Affair

As the Jewish community of America grew larger and stronger, it was able, more and more, to help the Jews who lived in the countries of the Old World. The bonds that linked the older Jewish community with the new one developing in America did not weaken as time went by. A common religion, common customs, a common history, common memories kept the Jews of the world united. They had, besides, always felt responsible for one another, one part of world Jewry coming to the defense of another when it was mistreated. The Jews of America, once dependent on their fellow Jews of the Old World for guidance and help, were now to become a strong force for preserving their persecuted people across the seas. For American freedom had given the impoverished, frightened immigrants of former days the ability to defend and help themselves when it was necessary.

In their secure homes in America, the Jews heard, time and again, of the mistreatment of their people in lands where persecution still reigned. In the year 1840, the world was startled by what came to be called the Damascus Affair. It had been a common device, among many rulers of the Old World, to divert the resentment of their subjects away from themselves toward the Jews. When a simple-minded peasant was told over and over again that it was the Jew who was to blame for his misery, he came in time to regard the Jew as the cause of all his ills. Many myths were created to make the Jew the object of fear and hatred. As the years went by and freedom grew, bringing more enlightenment to the people of the world, the myths began to fade into oblivion. In Damascus, however, as late as 1840, an ugly old falsehood claiming that Jews used Christian blood in the preparation of their Passover *matzah* again appeared in full bloom. Originally, the pagan Romans had accused the early Christians of using human blood. Later, the Christians directed the accusation against the Jews. Now, in Damascus, a monk, Father Thomas, disappeared. Despite their claim that they knew nothing of his disappearance, thirteen Jews were arrested on the charge that they had killed Father Thomas. Sixty Jewish children were seized and held without food, so as to wring confessions from their parents who, the officials hoped, would be willing to confess to anything rather than see their children suffer.

But this time the world did not let the accusation go unchallenged. Protests poured in from the civilized countries. In England, the Board of Delegates of British Jews asked its president, Moses Montefiore, who was also Sheriff of London, to go to Syria and speak to its ruler, Mehemet Ali. Adolphe Crémieux, a Jewish statesman of France, joined Moses Montefiore, as did Salomon Munk, an Orientalist who worked in the National Library of Paris. The result of the intervention was that nine Jews were freed, four having, in the meantime, died in prison as a result of the torture they had suffered. Not satisfied with a mere pardon, since the victim had committed no crime which needed to be pardoned, Montefiore succeeded in having the Sultan declare that the blood accusation was false. And Salomon Munk, the orientalist who understood Arabic, had the Sultan substitute the word "justice" for "mercy" in his statement exonerating the Jews.

In 1840, when the Damascus Affair took place, there were only about forty thousand Jews in the United States. Unlike the Jews of England, who had their Board of Delegates of British Jews to represent them, the Jews of America did not act as a single body. But they held protest meetings in New York, Baltimore and Philadelphia. At the meetings in New York and Philadelphia resolutions were drawn up and sent to President Martin Van Buren, asking for intervention in Damascus. It turned out, however, that the President had already intervened on behalf of the victims of Damascus.

Realizing the need for unity of action, and seeing how Moses Montefiore had gone to Syria as spokesman for all the Jews of England whose congregations were represented in the Board of Delegates of British Jews, Isaac Leeser tried, in 1841, to organize such a union in the United States. But it was not for a number of years, after new incidents in the Old World, and after the Jews grew more numerous in America, that such a union was achieved.

The Mortara Affair

In 1858 came another incident that shook the civilized world. A troop of Papal guards broke into the home of the Mortaras, a Jewish family in Bologna, Italy, and carried off six-year-old Edgar Mortara to be raised in a convent as a Catholic. When the incident was investigated it was found that when the child was two years old he had been ill, and his Catholic nurse, hoping to save him, had had him secretly baptized. Four years later she confessed what she had done, and the Pope, claiming that once a person was baptized he belonged to the Church, sent a troop of guards to seize the child.

Again a storm of protests arose, from Christians as well as Jews, as the distracted parents appealed for help. Again Moses Montefiore hastened to intervene, this time going to Italy to see the Pope. But the protests and outcries were of no avail. The Pope refused to surrender Edgar Mortara, and he was brought up as a Catholic.

The Mortara Affair made many Jews in America and France

realize that they must have representatives to speak for them whenever necessary, so that their defense of their people would be more
effective. Under the leadership of Adolphe Crémieux, the *Alliance
Israélite Universelle* was formed in France. And in America, a number of congregations united in the Board of Delegates of American
Israelites. But the Board of Delegates, which represented only a
small section of the Jews of America, lasted only until 1878, when
it merged with the Union of American Hebrew Congregations. The
time had still not come when the Jews of America were to unite
their forces under one authority which would speak for all of them
to the powers of the world.

Pogroms in Eastern Europe

As the nineteenth century drew to a close, and as the tyrannical rulers of the Old World felt the swell of rebellion shake their thrones, they tried to divert the anger of their subjects more and more to the defenseless Jews. In some lands, the Jews were so repressed by legal restrictions that they were reduced almost to pauperism. From poverty-stricken Romania, at the beginning of the twentieth century, thousands of Jews, unable to bear any longer their poverty and the restrictions they suffered, made their way to the harbor cities and sailed for America. Roused by the condition of the fugitives, John Hay, the American Secretary of State, addressed a note to the countries of Europe that had signed the Treaty of Berlin back in 1878. The treaty had provided that Romania, which had rebelled against Turkey, was to have her independence on condition that all her inhabitants would be granted civil and political rights. But Romania, John Hay pointed out, had not lived up to her obligations. ". . . These helpless people," he wrote, "burdened and spurned by their native land, are forced by the sovereign power of Romania upon the charity of the United States. This government cannot be a tacit party to such an international wrong. It is constrained to protest the treatment to which the Jews of Romania are subjected, not alone because it has unimpeachable rights to remonstrate against the resultant injury to itself, but in the name of humanity. . . ."

A year after John Hay wrote his note denouncing Romania's treatment of the Jews, a pogrom took place in Russia more ferocious and brutal than the Jews had ever suffered in that country. In April, 1903, drunken mobs, incited by higher authorities, were permitted to vent their rage on the Jews of the city of Kishineff. For two days the attackers did as they pleased, destroying homes, plundering, murdering. When the police did interfere, it was to disarm

a group of Jews who were trying to defend themselves. On the evening of the second day of the pogrom the governor of the province received a telegram, which he had been expecting, from the Minister of the Interior, one of the chief instigators of the pogrom. The telegram stated that it was time to stop the massacre. On receipt of the message, the governor suppressed the violence at once. When the carnage was over, it was found that forty-seven Jews had been killed, hundreds wounded, and thirteen hundred homes and shops destroyed. The highways were filled again with Jewish fugitives streaming toward safety beyond the borders of Russia. "Kishineff" became a rallying cry for Jews everywhere, the symbol of their suffering and of their need for a place of refuge. "We will not forget Kishineff," wrote Theodore Herzl, working for a homeland for his people in Palestine.

In 1905, when the revolution threatened to end the reign of the Czars, a new wave of pogroms was organized in Russia. And as had happened before, demonstrations and protest meetings were held in the civilized countries condemning the attacks upon the Jews. In the United States, a committee of Jews raised a million dollars to help the victims. In New York City, one hundred thousand men and women marched through the streets to the tolling of church bells.

The American Jewish Committee

In February, 1906, sixty leading Jews met in New York City to set up a Committee to protect Jewish rights wherever they were threatened. One of the founders of the Committee was Louis Marshall, a well-known lawyer who was active in public affairs and who was now also to become active in the affairs of his people. Most of the men who met to form the Committee were of German extraction, men who had become prominent on the American scene. The Jews from eastern Europe, more recent arrivals, had still not reached the prominence in public life of Jews who had come at an earlier date, but they too, in lesser degree, were represented on the Committee.

In November of the same year, the first meeting of the American Jewish Committee was held in New York City. Its delegates were selected by the founders of the Committee from each important community in the country.

Despite the fact that the Committee was not representative of all the Jews of America, it proved a valiant champion of Jewish rights in the coming years.

Abrogation of a Treaty

Back in 1832, the United States and Russia had made a treaty which, among other things, provided that the citizens of each country were to have the right to live "in all parts whatsoever" of the other. In 1866, an American citizen, on a visit to Russia, wanted to buy property in Kharkov. This right was denied him because he was a Jew. In 1880, another Jewish citizen of America was banished from St. Petersburg. In 1893, it was found that Russian consulates in the United States were denying visas to American Jews.

Resolutions were introduced in Congress time and again calling upon the President to denounce the Russian policy of discriminating against American Jews. But the discrimination continued for want of strong action on the part of the government. In 1907, the Secretary of State issued a statement saying that American Jews who had once been subjects of the Czar and who were travelling in Russia, put themselves under the jurisdiction of the laws of Russia. Therefore, the statement went on, the American Consulate could not issue passports to former Russian subjects or to Jews unless there was assurance from the government of Russia that they would be admitted. In his statement, the Secretary of State seemed to agree with Russia's claim that once a subject of the Czar, a man always remained a subject of the Czar. In addition, Jews who had not even been born in Russia were put under the jurisdiction of Russia's laws if they happened to be travelling in Russia.

The statement issued by the Secretary of State brought the newly-formed American Jewish Committee into the fight. Mayer Sulzburger, who was at that time president of the Committee, called upon the President to end the treaty with Russia since its provisions were being violated. Ending the treaty, however, meant ending important trade agreements, and this the government was unwilling to do. Conferences and discussions were held, month after month, but when these proved futile, the American Jewish Committee appealed to the public. The movement to end the treaty gained wider and wider support. Christians added their protests to those of the Jews. State Legislatures passed resolutions calling for abrogation of the treaty. Finally, unable to withstand the pressure of public opinion, the United States government ended its treaty with Russia in 1913.

The American Jewish Committee, leading the fight to abrogate the treaty, had achieved a victory not only for the Jews, but for the American principle of equal rights for all citizens.

World War

In 1914 the First World War broke out. On one side, when the war began, were the Allies, among them England, France and Russia. On the other side were the Central Powers, including Germany and Austria-Hungary. The war gradually spread, drawing other countries, including the United States, into the conflict.

When the United States entered the war, the Jews of America created a new organization, the Jewish Welfare Board, to serve the tens of thousands of Jewish boys in the fighting forces. Working under the supervision of the military authorities, the Jewish Welfare Board set up centers in France and in the war camps of America. Here the boys came for recreation, for religious services, for consultation with their chaplains. The Jewish Welfare Board did not disband when the war was over. It continued to maintain a military department, but its chief efforts were now directed toward the Jewish Center movement. In time, it became the central agency for the Jewish Y's and community centers, promoting their growth, providing them with programs and with trained personnel.

Until 1917 the United States remained neutral. During the years of America's neutrality, the war continued to rage in Europe. Since most of the Jews of Europe lived in the belligerent countries, they suffered all the hardships that went with the war. Increasingly, as time went by, Jewish leadership shifted from the Old World to the New, and the Jews of America assumed the responsibility of caring for their people overseas.

The large stretch of territory between Russia and the Central Powers, reaching from the Baltic Sea to the Black Sea, was known

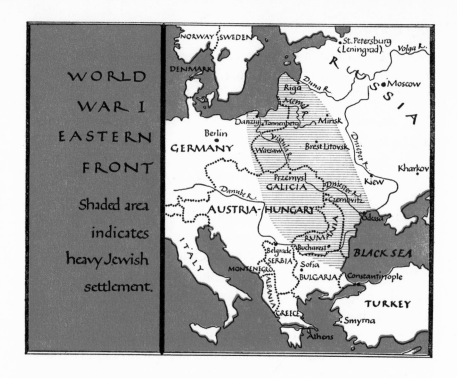

WORLD WAR I EASTERN FRONT

Shaded area indicates heavy Jewish settlement.

as the Eastern Front of the First World War. Here, in the lands of the Eastern Front, in Latvia, Lithuania, Poland, Galicia, the Ukraine, Romania, there lived about six million Jews. As war raged on the Eastern Front, as armies tramped back and forth, now advancing and now retreating and now digging in for battle, the civilian population, caught between the warring armies, suffered hunger, disease and homelessness. In addition, the Jews suffered the hostility of the Russian government. Though hundreds of thousands of Jews served in the armies of the Czar, fighting and dying for a country that had always persecuted them, the government, feeling that the Jews had reason to hope for her downfall, feared that they might help the enemy armies. Many times, therefore, the Russian High Command ordered that the Jews be moved farther east, into the interior, so that they could have no contact with the enemy. Thousands of Jews were deported from their homes, packed into boxcars and carried to an unknown destination.

The Joint Distribution Committee

In America, the Jews heard stories of what was happening on the Eastern Front. They read in their newspapers accounts of their native towns destroyed, of places from which they or their parents had come occupied by armies, of their people suffering hunger, stricken with disease, roaming the forests and highways in search of shelter. In 1917 came the Russian revolution, overthrowing the Czar and his government. In the confusion that followed the revolution, armies again marched back and forth over the countries of the Eastern Front, some of the armies consisting merely of bands of men who wanted to restore the Czar to the throne. Blaming the Jews for the downfall of the Czar, they attacked them at will, killing, looting, and instigating pogroms.

From the beginning of the war, the Jews of America had tried to bring some relief to their stricken people in the war zones. *Landsmanschaften* collected all the money they could and sent it to the survivors of their home towns. In 1914, the American Jewish Committee set up the American Jewish Relief Committee to collect funds to send overseas. Orthodox Jews organized another committee which they called the Central Committee for the Relief of Jewish War Sufferers. Still another committee, set up by workers, called itself the People's Relief Committee.

Though all the committees raised large sums of money, they soon realized that the distribution of funds should be a joint one, that is, that it should come from a common treasury and should go to the war victims according to their needs, regardless of their ideology. The committees therefore united, and so was born, in 1914, the American Joint Distribution Committee, often called Joint, or JDC.

The appeals for funds made by JDC reached every corner of the United States. Through newspapers, speakers, letters, and through personal appeal, JDC brought before the people of America a picture of what was happening in the lands of eastern Europe. "I bring you greetings from the starving nation," said Dr. Magnes to an audience after visiting Poland in 1915 for the JDC. "There are now two and a half million of our brethren in Poland, Lithuania and Galicia, hunger staring them in the face. Save the Jewish children who look to you for bread. The old men and the old women will pass away, and if this war continues longer, God knows how many of them will die in their tracks. But save these little children, that sing and play, this hope of our people, that have with them the possession of Judaism and the tradition of our long lineage of glory and hope. . . ."

Each year the sum collected by JDC mounted, six million in 1916, ten million in 1917. Between the years 1914 and 1924, fifty-nine million dollars was sent abroad by JDC. To bring help directly to the war victims, the JDC set up centers in the countries of the Eastern Front to administer the funds. The end of the war did not lessen the need for help, and the JDC used the money it collected to buy food, fight disease, build hospitals and clinics and homes. It set up schools where Jews could learn crafts they had never known, and it helped finance agricultural colonies for those who wanted to be farmers.

When the Second World War broke out, the Joint Distribution Committee again served the Jews overseas, during the war years and after, extending its relief and rehabilitation program into more and more lands. Through the JDC, the Jews of America were able to reach their people in the farthest corners of the world.

The American Jewish Congress

During the years of war, the Jews of America looked forward to the time when the war would end and when the nations of the world would send their representatives to discuss peace treaties.

They wanted to be sure there would be provisions, in the peace treaties, for equal rights for the Jews.

Even before the war ended, a movement began in the United States to set up an organization that would be more representative of the Jews of America than the American Jewish Committee, and that would speak, at the Peace Conference, for all the Jews of the country. More than three hundred thousand Jews from thousands of communities elected delegates to the American Jewish Congress, which was to work for "the attainment of full rights for Jews in all lands . . . and for the furtherance of Jewish interests in Palestine." The Congress chose delegates to go to Paris, where the Peace Conference was to take place. The American Jewish Committee also chose a delegation, headed by its president, Louis Marshall, to attend the Peace Conference. When the delegates arrived in Paris, they found delegations of Jews from England, France, and several other European countries. The delegations united, choosing Louis Marshall to be their chairman.

Minority Rights

Many of the countries of Europe had minorities, groups of people with a culture and a history that differed from the culture and history of the general population. In some European lands, these minorities, which had generally been conquered by the countries in which they lived, were not granted the civil and political rights enjoyed by the majority of the population.

The Jewish delegation, appearing before the Peace Conference, presented a plan for minority rights for the Jews of eastern Europe. According to the plan, the Jews were to have the right to their religion, customs, schools, language, institutions, and at the same time they were to enjoy the civil and political rights of the lands in which they lived.

The plan was adopted by the Peace Conference, not only for the Jews, but for other minorities as well. In the peace treaties drawn up for Poland, Romania, Hungary, minorities were guaranteed protection by their governments, and if the governments failed to live up to their responsibilities, the rights were guaranteed by the League of Nations.

Early in their history in America, the Jews of New Amsterdam had insisted on their civil rights, and so had helped other minorities win these rights. Now the Jews were insisting, on a world scale, that whatever rights were given to the general population should be given to them as well. And again, as had happened in New Amsterdam, their insistence on their rights helped other oppressed minorities to greater freedom.

The Continuing Struggle for Freedom

The need for self-defense organizations did not disappear with the end of the First World War. Even in a democratic country like the United States there were often outbursts of anti-Semitism. For prejudice, which had been permitted to flourish for hundreds of years, continued to find fertile soil to feed upon. And so the American Jewish Committee continued its work, as did the Anti-Defamation League of B'nai B'rith. Through pamphlets, through the radio, with whatever means they could use to educate the people, they fought the fight against anti-Semitism.

The American Jewish Congress, which, it was believed, would disband after the war, found that it must become a permanent body. One of the founders of the Congress, Rabbi Stephen S. Wise, served as its president for many years. With Rabbi Wise at its helm, leading, appealing to the public, conferring with political figures, the American Jewish Congress led many struggles to end discrimination against the Jews in America and to protect them in foreign lands.

Years passed, and in 1933 Adolf Hitler came to power in

Germany, overthrowing the Republic which had been set up after the First World War. With Hitler and the Nazis in control of the government, Germany was ruled through terror and murder. Proclaiming themselves the "master race," using the Jews as the scapegoat to be blamed for Germany's poverty, the Nazis drove the Jews from their professions, from their stores and industries. Thousands were thrown into prison, and thousands managed to flee the land.

Hoping to stave off the brutal blows against their people and to help stem the terror spreading from Germany to other lands, the American Jewish Congress called for a mass demonstration in New York's Madison Square Garden. At the same time, mass meetings were held in about three thousand other cities in the United States, Jews and Christians joining together in denouncing the Nazis. A movement was begun to boycott German goods, with the American Federation of Labor and the American Jewish Congress spreading the movement throughout the country. The boycott gained more and more supporters, reaching into thousands of American homes.

A few months after the demonstration in Madison Square Garden, when books written by Jewish authors were publicly burned

in Germany, the American Jewish Congress held a protest march in New York City, with Rabbi Wise and Nathan Straus leading the marchers. Then, in 1934, came a new group to help fight Nazism, the Jewish Labor Committee, whose supporters consist chiefly of men and women from the needle-trades industries.

But demonstrations, protests, public meetings, even boycott could not halt the Nazi drive for power. In 1939, Hitler, already having annexed Austria and Czechoslovakia, set out to conquer the world. He invaded Poland, thus starting the Second World War. To stop the Nazi menace, a number of countries united their forces. In time, the United States, England, France and Soviet Russia, among other countries, were ranged against Germany and her allies. For a long time Hitler's forces continued to gain ground, and in each country they conquered they set up concentration camps for the Jews and for other enemies of Nazism. The Jews, whom the Nazis wished to destroy completely, suffered the worst devastation they had ever known in their long history. Six million Jews were cold-bloodedly murdered by the men who called themselves the "master race."

With the destruction of the oldest and largest Jewish communities of Europe, the Jewish community of America became the largest and strongest in the world. In its new role of leadership, it found itself facing greater responsibilities than ever before. Most of the Jewish survivors of the war in Europe wanted to go to Palestine, where they felt they would at last find peace and freedom. It became the task of the Jews of America to bring relief and rehabilitation to the Jews remaining in Europe, and to help make Palestine a haven for those who wanted to migrate to the land of their fathers.

Things to Read

Alofsin, Dorothy, *The Stream of Jewish Life,* Union of American Hebrew Congregations, Cincinnati, 1943.

Berkowitz, Henry J., *Boot Camp,* Jewish Publication Society, Philadelphia, 1948.

Berkowitz, Henry J., *The Fire Eater,* Jewish Publication Society, 1941.

Leonard, Oscar, *Americans All,* "He Charley McCarthey'd Them," pp. 216-220; "He Saved the Lost Battalion," pp. 221-229.

Lusie, Rose G., *The Great March,* "The Second Purim," pp. 103-115.

Pessin, Deborah, *Giants on the Earth,* "Rise, Sir Moses," pp. 35-44.

Questions to Discuss

Despite the American ideals of freedom, prejudice and anti-Semitism did not completely disappear. Why not?

Why was prejudice against the Jews less likely to flourish in America than in lands like Syria and Russia, where poverty and ignorance prevailed?

Things to Do

Send to the Filmstrip House, 15 West 46th Street, New York 36, N.Y., for the filmstrip, "Free to Be Different."

Write to the American Jewish Committee, 386 4th Avenue, New York 16, N.Y., to the American Jewish Congress, 15 East 84th Street, New York 28, N.Y., and to the Anti-Defamation League of the B'nai B'rith, 212 Fifth Avenue, New York 10, N.Y., for material describing the work they are doing.

Teachers Bibliography

Handlin, Oscar, *Adventure in Freedom,* pp. 174-210.
Learsi, Rufus, *The Jews in America,* pp. 79-89; 217-356.
Lebeson, Anita, *Pilgrim People,* pp. 376-406.
Wise, Stephen S., *Challenging Years,* G. P. Putnam's Sons, New York, 1949.

CHAPTER 2

America and Israel

Memories

In the year 70 the Roman legions destroyed the Temple in Jerusalem. As the second Jewish Commonwealth came to an end, thousands of Jews fled to other lands. And slowly, as the years went by, the land of milk and honey became a land of desolation. Hot winds blew in from the desert, and there was no one to fight their destructiveness. Waves rolled in from the sea, leaving, in their wake, layer upon layer of sand, till there were only sand dunes where once there had been green meadows. Rain swept the good earth into the valleys and left the soil rocky and barren. The fields that had once yielded for the Children of Israel wheat and barley and rye turned into marshland. City walls crumbled and fell into decay. The land slept, desolate and deserted and silent.

But the exiles did not forget their little homeland on the edge of the Mediterranean. They scattered to every corner of the world, but they remembered Zion. Some grew prosperous, finding security and satisfaction in the new lands in which they dwelt. But it did not matter. They could not forget the land of King David and Solomon, the land of their prophets. They prayed for the Messiah to come and lead them back to Zion. "Sound the great horn for our freedom," they prayed. "Raise the ensign to gather our exiles." "Gather us from the four corners of the earth. . . ."

237

Centuries went by. Jackals roamed the bare hillsides of Judea. Lizards basked on the hot stones of the wasteland of Israel. Within the old walls of Jerusalem, a handful of Jews, clinging to their homeland, lived in dark little hovels. Bedouins came in from the desert and pitched their tents on the few green spots still left in the land. Here and there Arab peasants put up mud huts and scratched the soil with their primitive wooden plows. And in the lands of their dispersion, the Jews could not forget Zion. "Next year in Jerusalem," they kept telling one another every Passover, year after year, generation after generation. "Next year in Jerusalem." Old people, wishing to spend their last days in the land of their forefathers, made their way to Palestine, to live quietly within the crumbling walls of Jerusalem. And from all over the world, Jews sent money to support the few thousands of their people living in the land of memories.

Dreams of Zion in America

Like the Jews in every land, the Jews of America had always carried with them the dream of restoration to Palestine. The freedom and security they enjoyed in America did not lessen their love for the land of their fathers. From time to time, making the long, dangerous voyage across the sea, *sh'liḥim,* messengers from Palestine, came to the early Jewish settlers of the New World for money to help support the Jews living in Palestine. And like their people in every land, the Jews of America gave their contributions to the *sh'liḥim* to support the few Jews inhabiting Palestine.

It had been a custom of pious Jews through the ages to bury their dead with a small bag of earth brought from Palestine placed under the head. This custom, practiced by the Jews of America, was observed by a Christian historian in the city of Charleston. "It is a token of their remembrance of the Holy Land," he wrote in

1796, "and of their expectations of returning thither in God's appointed time."

Ezra Stiles, the pastor of Newport, also observed among the Jews indications of their love of Palestine, and of their expectation of the Messiah who would gather all of Israel and lead them back to the land of their fathers. "The Jews are wont in Thunder Storms to set open all their Doors & Windows for the coming of Messias," wrote Ezra Stiles in his diary. "Last Hail Storm 31 July, when Thunder, Rain and Hail were amazingly violent, the Jews of Newport threw open Doors, Windows, and employed themselves in Singing & repeating prayers, &c., for meeting Messiah."

Ezra Stiles liked nothing better than conversing with a rabbi, and one of his favorite subjects was the Messiah. Once it was with Rabbi Isaac Ḥayyim Karigal, a rabbi of the Old World who had come to visit Newport, that he formed a friendship. "This afternoon I spent with the Rabbi. . . ." wrote Ezra Stiles. "I asked him when he expected the Messiah. He said daily, probably within about forty years. . . ."

The idea of restoration to Palestine had become so basic to Judaism that it continued to flourish even in America, where the persecution the Jews had suffered in the Old World was only a memory. And though they might not themselves have expected to return, they still saw it as the ancient homeland of their people. Thus Mordecai Noah, in 1825, eager to bring relief to his oppressed people in the Old World, had tried to establish a state for them on Grand Island, a temporary homeland till they could finally return to Palestine. The Jews of the Old World did not respond to Noah's invitation to come to Grand Island, and Noah turned his thoughts more and more to Palestine itself, and to how it should be colonized by the returning Jews. About twenty years after his effort to establish a Jewish state in America, he presented a plan, which was widely circulated, for the colonization of the Holy Land. ". . . The whole territory surrounding Jerusalem . . . will be occupied by enterprising Jews. The valleys of the Jordan will be filled by agriculturists from the north of Germany, Poland and Russia. Merchants will occupy the seaports. . . . Those who desire to reside in the Holy Land and have not the means will be aided by societies to reach their desired haven of repose."

While Mordecai Noah dreamed and planned, and while the Jews of America built ever greater security, the situation of the Jews in eastern Europe continued to grow worse, and the movement for a return to Zion grew stronger. In the late nineteenth century, when the pogroms and the May Laws of Russia drove thousands of Jews to the shores of America, the refugees brought with them the ideals of Zionism. The societies called *Hov'vei Zion,* Lovers of Zion, which had sprung up in Russia and Poland, were also organized in America by the east European Jews. But because these later immigrants were occupied for a long time with adjusting themselves to America and with learning to earn a living, the societies remained scattered and few in number.

Going Up

From Russia, in the meantime, small groups of pioneers, members of BILU, were migrating to Palestine. They would begin to restore the homeland, they said, and others would follow. They went hungry and thirsty as they worked on the stony soil of Palestine, and many grew ill with malaria. Some of them, unable to bear the hardships, returned to the land of the Czars. Some managed to dig in, but tired of the struggle, hired cheap Arab labor to help develop their patches of land. Some never lost courage. Like all pioneers, they resolved to conquer the wilderness.

From 1905 to 1914, when the First World War broke out, there came a new, a larger wave of settlers, a new *Aliyah,* a "going up." This time not a handful, but thousands of pioneers, or *halutzim,* came to Palestine, most of them from eastern Europe. They broke

stones for roads, and they built the roads. They drained miles of marshland and broke through the stubborn, neglected soil. When the ground had been broken they planted seed. They planted trees to hold the soil in place. And gradually, life began to stir in the wilderness.

The *ḥalutzim* came to Palestine with the thought of redeeming the land not only for themselves, but for all their people. And because they did not want a society where one man worked for another, they built cooperative settlements, *kibbutzim,* some plowing, some building, some caring for the chickens, some for the livestock, some for the gardening.

Growth of Zionism in America

As the members of BILU and later the *ḥalutzim* toiled on the soil, the movement of Zionism grew, gaining new followers everywhere. In America, for a while, support of Zionism came chiefly from the east European Jews, but gradually the idea of a Jewish homeland in Palestine began to stir the imagination of other sections of American Jewry. In 1897, Theodor Herzl, arranging for the first World Zionist Congress, wrote in his diary, "The movement is starting in America." That same year, when the Congress was called, American Jewry, the youngest in the world, responded to the call. A delegation of American Zionists sailed for Basle, Switzerland, to participate in the discussions of the World Zionist Congress. The following year, in 1898, the Federation of American Zionists, an organization which was to become, in 1918, the Zionist Organization of America, was founded.

Growth of the Federation continued slowly at first. Still supported chiefly by east European Jews, "western" Jews hesitated for a long time before joining the ranks, though many leaders of the Federation were of German descent. It was not till prominent men Like Louis Brandeis, a Justice of the United States Supreme Court, joined and helped lead the movement, that the Zionist ranks began to swell. By the time the First World War broke out, Zionism had become strong enough in America to extend ever greater help to the *Yishuv*, the settlement of Palestine.

Help From America

When the First World War engulfed the countries of Europe, Palestine was under Turkish rule. Oppressed by Turkish officials who taxed and harassed them, the Jews of Palestine, now numbering about a hundred thousand, were pro-British. Turkey, fighting on the side of Germany, was hostile to the *Yishuv*. People were arrested, thrown into prison, tortured, expelled from the land. The war blockade, in addition, shut off the *Yishuv* from foreign markets, so that the wine, oranges and almonds being produced in Palestine could not be sold abroad, or exchanged for other goods. With the Jews of Europe embroiled in the war, with America still neutral and the Jews of America grown to be the richest Jewish community in the world, the Jews of the old-new community of Palestine turned to their people in the New World for help.

Meeting in New York City in the summer of 1914, Zionist delegates set up the Provisional Executive Committee for General Zionist Affairs. The Committee, headed by Brandeis, now the leader of the movement in America, sent out a call for two-hundred thousand dollars. Ten months later, three-hundred and fifty thousand dollars was sent to the *Yishuv*. Persuaded by Zionist leaders, President Wilson and the Secretary of the Navy permitted the use of battleships and colliers to carry food and money to the thousands of people in the *Yishuv* facing starvation. But Palestine, struggling grimly for its life, drew support not only from the Zionists. In 1915 an American collier, the *Vulcan*, sailed into the harbor of Jaffa with nine hundred tons of goods, sent by the Zionists of America and by the American Jewish Committee.

One of the most important of the Zionist organizations of America was Hadassah, which had been founded by Henrietta Szold, daughter of Rabbi Benjamin Szold of Baltimore. Henrietta Szold had visited Palestine in 1912, and as she journeyed through the land, she was dismayed at the widespread illness and poverty she found everywhere. The native population, Jews and Arabs, suffered from trachoma and malaria. In their unsanitary surroundings in the old cities, without doctors, nurses, hospitals, clinics, the diseases went unchecked, and the simplest rules of hygiene were unknown. The Jewish pioneers who had come to Palestine also fell victims to malaria, the disease bred in the swamps they had come to drain. Determined to bring health to Palestine, Henrietta Szold returned to America and founded Hadassah.

In 1916, the Provisional Committee gave Hadassah the task of organizing a health unit for Palestine. With its branches all over the country, Hadassah swung into action. One morning in 1918, twelve camouflaged warships left New York harbor with thousands of troops for the war areas of Europe. Among the troops were forty-four men and women wearing red stars of David. They were on their way to Palestine, sent by Hadassah, to begin their health program.

The Balfour Declaration

On November 2, 1917, a year before the close of the war, England issued the Balfour Declaration. "His Majesty's government view with favor the establishment in Palestine of a national home for the Jewish people, and will use their best endeavors to facilitate the achievement of this object, it being clearly understood that nothing shall be done which may prejudice the civil and religious rights of existing non-Jewish communities in Palestine, or the rights and political status enjoyed by Jews in any other country."

The tidings of the Balfour Declaration swept through the world, overwhelming the Jews with the miracle of it. What they had hungered and wept for over the centuries would at last be theirs. In America, the Jews held celebrations all over the land. They were aware of the part their Zionist leaders had played in the issuance of

the Balfour Declaration. Had she not had the approval of the American government, England would not have issued the declaration. It had therefore been the task of the American Zionists to win, for Zionism, the support of the government and of the President of the United States. American Zionists had made themselves heard, in the newspapers and at meetings. Zionist leaders like Stephen S. Wise and Louis D. Brandeis, who were close to President Wilson, had discussed with him the importance of a declaration restoring their ancient homeland to the Jews. Seeing the justice of the Zionist cause and responding to public opinion, Wilson had declared himself in favor of the Zionist ideals, and in 1917, England issued the Balfour Declaration. The League of Nations gave England the mandate for Palestine. Thus ended Turkish rule in Palestine, and a new era began for the *Yishuv* and for the Zionist movement in America.

Growth of the Yishuv

The Balfour Declaration brought thousands of new *halutzim* to Palestine. Many more miles of marshland were drained and restored to fertility. Cooperatives multiplied. The shacks of the early pioneers gave way to trim, red-roofed cottages. Tractors moved over the fields. The Jewish National Fund, created by the World Zionist Organization, collected money from Jews the world over to buy land from Arab landlords. Most of the money came from the Jews of America, because they had more to give. Not only Zionist funds poured into Palestine. Between 1917 and 1924, the Joint Distribution Committee spent three million dollars in the *Yishuv*.

And so Palestine bloomed again. Industry began to flourish. Tel-Aviv, built on sand dunes, was a town of fifteen hundred residents in 1914. Ten years later it had a population of twenty-five thousand. Haifa became one of the most important harbor cities on the Mediterranean. Pioneers came to Palestine from America and built cooperatives, sharing the hardships of all other *halutzim* who had come to the land. In 1925 the Hebrew University opened on Mount Scopus in the city of Jerusalem. All over the United States, Jewish communities celebrated the opening of the university, the fulfilment of a dream that Palestine would become a center of culture. An organization was formed in America, Friends of the Hebrew University, to raise funds which would support and develop the new institution. Leadership too came from America when Dr. Judah Magnes went to Palestine to become Chancellor of the Hebrew University.

Conflict in the Yishuv

But despite all the help they received, many obstacles beset the *halutzim* rebuilding the old homeland. Not all the Arabs were friendly to the developing *Yishuv*. Many Arab landlords, living on the labor of Arab peasants, did not want to see a flourishing state in Palestine where people lived contentedly in collectives. They feared that the Arab peasants might learn to prefer the way of life developing in the collectives, where all shared alike the fruit of their labors. There was also a group of Arabs who wanted Palestine to be a national home for their own people, rather than for the Jews. Nor were all the British officials friendly to the *Yishuv*. There were many millions of Arabs in Syria, Transjordan, Iraq, Egypt, Arabia, while the Jews of Palestine were numbered only in the thousands. Friendship with the Arabs, they felt, would mean a market for English goods, and rights to Arab oil fields.

To rouse the Arab peasants against the Jews, Arab leaders spread rumors that the Jews, wishing to destroy Mohammedanism, were attacking their holy places. Led by agents sent to incite them, Arabs rioted against the Jews in 1920, in 1921, and again in 1929. The British government, using the riots as an excuse to halt the development of the *Yishuv*, issued a White Paper in 1929 limiting Jewish immigration to Palestine and prohibiting the Jews from buying more land. But world protest was so strong that the White Paper was withdrawn, and the *Yishuv* continued to grow.

In 1939, after three years of Arab riots and in the very year when the Second World War broke out, Great Britain issued another White Paper, sharply reducing immigration to Palestine. Hundreds of thousands of Jews in Europe, borne down upon by the Nazi monster, found the door of the promised Jewish homeland closed in their faces. To satisfy Arab nationalist leaders who, the English feared, might help the Nazis, the British government did all she could to appease them. The Jews, the British knew, did not need appeasement to ensure their loyalty, for they were bitter enemies of the Nazis, who were destroying their people in Europe.

With the outbreak of the Second World War, the Jews of Palestine had two enemies to fight, the Nazis as well as the White Paper. "We will fight beside Great Britain," declared the *Yishuv*, "as though there were no White Paper, and we will fight the White Paper as though there were no war."

Fighting the White Paper

Although Palestine was not officially in the war, many thousands of men and women enrolled for service in Britain's armies. And as they had promised, while fighting beside Great Britain, the Jews also fought the White Paper. They dropped parachutists behind enemy lines to rescue as many Jews as possible through underground channels. The *Haganah,* the Jewish defense force of Palestine, helped thousands of Jews enter Palestine without certificates of entry. *Ma'apilim,* these new immigrants were called, "those who advance against great obstacles." But not all the *ma'apilim* who set out for Palestine reached her shores. British planes, cruisers and destroyers patrolled the waters of the Mediterranean, on the lookout for vessels bringing refugees to Palestine. Often the little vessels were caught and the passengers, within reach at last of the one land eager to receive them, were sent back to Europe or held in detention camps. But the *Haganah,* as the war went on, learned how to evade the planes and cruisers and destroyers. Through underground channels, the *Haganah* learned when a vessel bringing refugees was to arrive. Often, on the night before the arrival, members of the *Haganah* blew up British radar and coastal guard stations along the seacoast. And as the vessel slipped through the waters, members of *Haganah* brought the *ma'apilim* ashore in their own small boats, or swam out and returned to shore with them on their backs.

From far overseas, the Jews of America joined in the fight to open the doors of Palestine and to help the remnant of their people who had survived the onslaught of the Nazis. The United Palestine Appeal and the Joint Distribution Committee united their forces in the United Jewish Appeal. Called upon to help save the *Yishuv* and the Jews still remaining in Europe, the Jews of America oversubscribed the one-hundred-million dollar quota set by the United Jewish Appeal. The following year the United Jewish Appeal col-

lected one-hundred and seventy-million dollars for the *Yishuv* and
for reconstruction work in Europe and in North Africa.

The coming of Hitler to power, the struggle of the *Yishuv* against
the White Paper, the fate of six million Jews in Europe, swelled the
ranks of the Zionist movement in America. But not only Zionists
were concerned with the *Yishuv* and with the Jews trying to reach
Palestine. The American Jewish Committee and the American Jewish Congress joined the Zionist groups in protests against the White
Paper. Lodges, labor organizations, rabbinical associations, demanded that the White Paper be withdrawn. The Zionist groups
closed their ranks in the American Zionist Emergency Council, the
better to organize help for the *Yishuv*. With the Emergency Council as the parent body, hundreds of small emergency councils were
organized all over the United States to rouse public opinion against
the White Paper. So well did the councils do their work, that protests kept flooding the American government, from Jews and Chris-

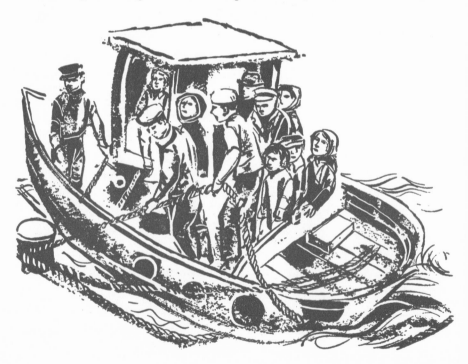

tians, from people in every walk of life. State governors and members of Congress sent in resolutions denouncing the White Paper. Thousands of Christians formed an American Palestine Committee, while more than two thousand clergymen joined in a Christian Council for Palestine.

Nor did the Jews of America sit by and watch the struggle of the *Yishuv* to bring *ma'apilim* to Palestine. Groups were organized in America to gather supplies, to get ships for bringing refugees from the Nazi-dominated lands to Palestine, and to recruit crews to man the ships. *Exodus 1947, Haganah, Theodor Herzl* and other ships were sent by the Jews of America, manned by American Jews and Christians, to bring *ma'apilim* to Palestine.

Led by Henrietta Szold, who had made her home in Palestine, Hadassah threw all its energies into the Youth Aliyah movement, the movement to bring Jewish children from Europe to Palestine. The movement was begun by Henrietta Szold in 1934, and by 1945, seventeen thousand children had been brought to the *Yishuv*. Youth *Aliyah* continued even after the war ended, for peace could not bring back to the children their parents who had been killed. By 1954, Palestine had gathered sixty-two thousand children. She had

brought them through the underground railroads, over mountain and sea, and Hadassah, with its supplies and funds flowing into the *Yishuv,* helped restore them to a normal life in the collective settlements.

The war ended at last. Hitler was defeated and civilization raised its head amid the ruins. Of the millions of Jews who had lived in Europe before the war, only thousands were left. Their homes gone, their relatives killed, the lives they had built shattered, most of them wanted to go to Palestine, to the land always ready to welcome them. There was still strife in Palestine between the Arabs and Jews and there was still the White Paper denying them entrance. But they wanted to go "home."

The Partition Plan

Unwilling to cope with the situation any longer, Great Britain placed the problem of Palestine before the United Nations. The United Nations appointed a committee to go to Palestine and talk to Arabs and Jews, and to suggest a solution for the problem. When the committee returned, in 1947, it suggested that Great Britain give up the mandate, and that Palestine be partitioned into two states, a Jewish State and an Arab State, while Jerusalem be internationalized and put under the control of the United Nations. For a year longer, England was to keep the mandate and maintain peace in Palestine. The Partition Plan was acceptable to the *Yishuv,* but was rejected by the Arab leaders.

For several months the United Nations considered the Partition Plan, while the Jews of America did all they could to rouse public opinion in its favor. Though the American delegation in the United Nations had declared itself in favor of the Plan, it kept vacillating in the General Assembly, now favoring the Jews and now the Arabs. Alarmed at the attitude of the American delegation which had

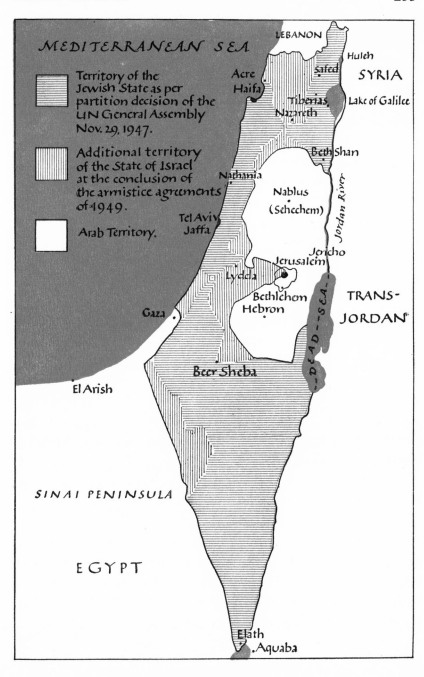

MEDITERRANEAN SEA

Territory of the
Jewish State as per
partition decision of the
UN General Assembly
Nov. 29, 1947.

Additional territory
of the State of Israel
at the conclusion of
the armistice agreements
of 1949.

Arab Territory.

LEBANON

Huleh

Acre
Haifa

Safed

SYRIA

Tiberias
Nazareth

Lake of Galilee

Beth Shan

Nathania

Nablus
(Schechem)

Jordan River

Tel Aviv
Jaffa

Jericho
Jerusalem

Lydda

Bethlehem
Hebron

DEAD SEA

TRANS-
JORDAN

Gaza

Beer Sheba

DEAD SEA

El Arish

SINAI PENINSULA

EGYPT

Elath
Aquaba

great influence in the United Nations, the Zionist groups sent their best spokesmen to argue the cause of the *Yishuv,* to speak to the delegations of the United Nations. But the Zionists were not alone in the struggle to help create a Jewish state in Palestine. Other Jewish groups added their strength, appealing for American and world support. Giving way before the pressure of public opinion, the American delegation joined with the majority of the nations in voting for the Partition Plan. When the United Nations announced its decision, there was dancing and singing and weeping for joy among the Jews of the world. True, tiny Palestine was to be divided, but there would be a Jewish homeland, however small, approved by the United Nations.

Israel Reborn

But even while the Jews rejoiced, Arab riots broke out in Palestine, for the Arab leaders were not content with just a part of Palestine. Then, from the neighboring Arab states, from Egypt, Iraq, Saudi Arabia, Transjordan, Syria, Lebanon, a steady infiltration began. Arabs came in as "irregulars," well-trained and armed for war. Though the "irregulars" were pouring in by the thousands, the British Administration declared the *Haganah,* the Jewish defense army, illegal, and ordered it disbanded.

As the situation grew more tense in Palestine, with the *Haganah* fighting off the Arab bands, the United States suggested that instead of instituting the Partition Plan, the country be put under the trusteeship of the United Nations. But the *Yishuv* refused. It wanted its independence. In New York City, forty thousand Jewish war veterans marched down Fifth Avenue in protest against the American government's proposal, while special services were held in synagogues all over the country.

In May, 1948, the British mandate ended and the British High Commissioner sailed for England. On the afternoon of his sailing,

on May 14, David ben Gurion read his people's declaration of independence. ". . . we, the members of the National Council, representing the Jewish people in Palestine and the Zionist movement of the world, . . . hereby proclaim the establishment of the Jewish state in Palestine, to be called Israel. . . ."

The day after the declaration was read, armies from seven Arab lands began to pour into Palestine. Settlements and roads were fired upon from the hills. Jerusalem was besieged. The Jews did not have the equipment of the Arabs, the planes, the artillery, the tanks. But they had, said David ben Gurion, head of the Jewish Agency, a secret weapon, the will to be free.

And again, from the Jews of America, came help for the defenders of the Jewish state. Since America and Britain had imposed an embargo on the shipment of arms to Palestine, they smuggled whatever they could into the land, arms, medical supplies, vaccines. American Jewish veterans of the war, particularly air pilots, fought with their people in Israel in defense of their independence. David Marcus, a Colonel in the American army and a veteran of the Second World War, was given supreme command of the Jerusalem sector. Marcus was killed by an enemy bullet and his body was brought back to the United States, to be buried at West Point with full military honors. And in Israel, a road built in the dark of night, over hills and precipices, was named Marcus Road, in honor of the American who had given his life for his people. And not only Jews from America, but Christians too, helped repel the invaders. The volunteers from America were few in number compared with the many thousands of defenders in Israel, but their courage and their very presence encouraged the Jews of the *Yishuv,* for they felt they were not alone.

Outnumbered, poorly equipped, the miracle that had taken place in the days of the Maccabees was repeated in the reborn state of Israel. The defenders gained the offensive. The Arabs were driven out of Galilee, out of the Negev, out of the wide corridor leading to Jerusalem.

In January, 1949, an armistice was signed and the war was over. That month Israel held its elections, with Jews and Arabs alike voting at the polls for their representatives to the Constituent Assembly. The two thousand years of waiting were at an end. Israel was again a nation. And the Jews of America, who had worked and struggled to make the dream come true, rejoiced with their brother community in the ancient homeland.

Things to Read

Hoffman, Gail, *The Land and the People of Israel,* J. P. Lippincott Co., New York, 1950.
Levinger, Elma Ehrlich, *Fighting Angel,* Behrman House, New York, 1946.
Pessin, Deborah, *Theodor Herzl,* Behrman House, New York, 1948.
Zeligs, Dorothy, *The Story of Modern Israel,* Bloch Publishing Co., New York, 1950.

Questions to Discuss

Why did Zionism find its strongest supporters at first among East European Jews?

Why did the movement of Zionism grow stronger in America after the coming of Hitler?

Why did the Jews of America feel responsible for saving the *Yishuv?*

Things to Do

Write to the branch of Hadassah in your city for whatever material is available on its work in Israel.

Write to the Department of Education and Culture, Jewish Agency, 16 East 66th Street, New York 21, N.Y., for the filmstrips "This Is Israel" and "Galilee."

Teachers Bibliography

Bentwich, Norman, *For Zion's Sake,* Jewish Publication Society, Philadelphia, 1954.
Lebeson, Anita, *Pilgrim People,* pp. 407-507.
Samuel, Maurice, *Harvest in the Desert,* Jewish Publication Society, Philadelphia, 1944.

CHAPTER **3**

Builders in the
Golden Land

From their drab ghettoes, from the shabby villages of the Pale, from every hamlet and city and province and country where they had suffered tyranny and persecution, the Jews had looked to America, which they called the "Golden Land." Beyond the sneers, the threats, the voices raised in fury, the taunts following them down the streets, the doors of universities closed in their faces, beyond the howling mobs, the pogroms, the expulsions, the torture, the criminal attacks, beyond all these they saw America, the Golden Land.

America received them, and gratefully, they gave her their gifts. They gave her their talents, their creativeness, their ideals, their dreams for the future. They came when America was still a wilderness, and they helped build civilization. They enriched American life with their culture, with their Bible, their idiom and literature.

Their talents developed in the Golden Land. Restricted in the Old World, they were free to do what they chose in the New World. So Judah Touro was a merchant and Mordecai Noah was a politician and Myer Myers was a silversmith. As the years went by and their numbers grew and freedom became as familiar as the ground they walked upon, their creativity went out in every direction. Denied the right to cultivate the soil in the Old World, David Lubin, born in eastern Europe, became identified with the soil in the New World. For a time he ran a store in Sacramento, California. Trading with the farmers, he learned to understand their problems, their difficulties in getting their products to the markets of the cities at a cost which would still leave them a profit. When David Lubin became a fruit grower, he organized the California Fruit Growers Exchange, so that the fruit growers could send their fruit to the markets collectively, thus keeping down the cost of transportation. David Lubin continued to work for the protection of the farmer, arguing for government subsidies to compensate for the cost of transportation to foreign markets. His ideas spread, and in Philadelphia fifty-five clergymen formed a "Lubin Club." Articles were written on the need for protecting the farmer. "Lubinism" became a word known throughout the land. Realizing that farmers all over the world faced the same problems, high cost of transportation and competition, David Lubin went to Europe, hoping to persuade the nations of the world to cooperate on behalf of the farmers. Finally, in 1905, under the sponsorship of King Victor Emmanuel III, the representatives of forty nations met in Rome, where they established the International Institute of Agriculture, with David Lubin as its head. Twenty-five years after his death in Rome, seventy nations sent representatives to honor the memory of the man who had worked for harmony among the nations of the world.

Jewish benefactors to mankind grew more and more numerous in the Golden Land. Attracted since earliest days to the art of healing, the Jews developed doctors of medicine, the general practitioner, the specialist, the doctor who sought the cure for disease through science. Casimir Funk discovered vitamins. Bela Schick developed the Schick test for determining one's susceptibility to diphtheria. Joseph Goldberger devoted himself to discovering the cause and cure of pellagra. Jonas E. Salk developed the Salk polio vaccine, lifting from parents and children the fear of the crippling disease.

They produced scientists and inventors. Charles P. Steinmetz, the electrical "wizard," contributed to the physical sciences. Isaac Singer invented the sewing machine. Franz Boas was a world-famous anthropologist. When Albert Einstein, discoverer of the laws of relativity, was cast out by Germany, his native land, he was welcomed by the Golden Land, and became one of her favorite sons.

To the Golden Land came Lazarus Straus in 1854, bringing three young sons, Isidor, Nathan and Oscar. Isidor became a member of Congress. Oscar served as American minister to Turkey under Presidents Cleveland, McKinley and Taft. Under President Theodore Roosevelt, he served as Secretary of Commerce and Labor. "Oh, that we had more like him," said President Truman. "I wish we could raise more of the same stock." The third son of Lazarus Straus, Nathan, lived in a country home where he enjoyed the produce of his own farm. One day Nathan Straus' cow fell sick, so that the milk was contaminated and could not be drunk. Nathan Straus had heard of Louis Pasteur, the French scientist who had developed the process of pasteurization, which purified milk. Nathan Straus saw the importance of pasteurized milk, the many lives that could be saved if only pure milk was used. But it was not an easy matter to convince the milk companies to change their method of handling milk. It meant keeping their dairies clean, inspection of their cows, new machinery, and therefore greater costs. For twenty years Nathan Straus carried on a campaign for clean dairies and milk inspection. At last laws were passed requiring that milk be inspected, and in some places, the laws required that it be pasteurized. But as a result of the attention now being given to milk, its price went up, and many poor people could not afford to buy it. Nathan Straus, a rich man, then set up milk stations in New York City where milk was sold to the poor below cost, and distributed free of charge to those who could not afford to buy it at all. Not satisfied with confining his work to America, and because he was devoted to the Zionist cause, Nathan Straus set up a Pasteur Institute in Palestine, as well as a Health Center in the city of Jerusalem.

Lovers of justice as they were of healing, the Jews of the Golden Land produced great jurists. Louis D. Brandeis, who defended the interests of the common man against the rich companies, was known as the "people's lawyer." He became a Justice of the Supreme Court. "Isaiah," Franklin Delano Roosevelt called him, because he loved justice. Benjamin Nathan Cardozo, a great grandson of Rabbi Seixas of revolutionary days, was also a Justice of the Supreme Court. Gentle, scholarly, wise, the students of Columbia Law School, where he studied, called him "Nathan the Wise." Felix Frankfurter, who began by selling newspapers on the sidewalks of New York, became a professor of law at Harvard University, then a Justice of the Supreme Court.

The horizons reached far and wide in the Golden Land. Herbert Lehman served as Governor and Senator of New York, and Moses Alexander as Governor of Idaho, and Abraham Ribicoff as Governor of Connecticut. Jesse Isidor Straus served as Ambassador to

France, and Lewis L. Strauss as Chairman of the Atomic Energy Commission. These men, like the doctors, the lawyers, the professors, the scientists, were but a few of the many.

Democracy did not say, as did tyranny in the Old World, you cannot serve if you are a Jew. Democracy did not restrict the Jews to selling old clothes, or to petty trading. They could, if they wished, be masons, carpenters, teamsters, ferrymen, real estate agents, school teachers, engineers, soldiers, machinists, dentists, deans of

colleges, psychiatrists. They could, like Bernard Baruch, be men whom presidents invited for quiet fireside chats, so that they could discuss the affairs of state. Bernard Baruch, son of immigrants to the New World, was first appointed, in 1916, by President Wilson to the position of member of the Council of National Defense. Such ability did Bernard Baruch have for administrative work, and so well did he know the country and its industries, that Wilson soon gave him a more responsible position, Chairman of the War Industries Board, so that he could mobilize the industries of the country toward winning the war. Bernard Baruch served under President after President, year after year, in public office or behind the scenes, counselling, planning, marshalling the facts, pointing out the steps to take and the course to follow, so that in time he came to be called the "elder statesman."

The Golden Land was a land of developing culture, of music, painting, literature. So many Jews became great musicians. Jascha Heifetz, Efrem Zimbalist, Mischa Elman, Nathan Milstein, Yehudi Menuhin, Artur Rubinstein, George Gershwin, Benny Goodman,

Bruno Walter, Leonard Bernstein, Aaron Copland, Ernest Bloch, Jerome Kern, Richard Rodgers. . . . And they wrote books and plays and poetry. Lillian Hellman, Arthur Miller, Elmer Rice, Sidney Kingsley, Moss Hart, Samuel N. Behrman, Herman Wouk, Robert Nathan, Ludwig Lewisohn, Maurice Samuel, Meyer Levin, Louis Untermeyer, Babette Deutsch, Muriel Rukeyser. . . . And they painted. Leon Kroll, Max Weber, Jack Levine, Ben Shahn, Raphael Soyer. . . . And they were sculptors. William Zorach, Jo Davidson. . . . And they were actors. Paul Muni, Joseph Schildkraut, Al Jolson, Charlie Chaplin, the Marx Brothers, Danny Kaye, Sylvia Sidney, Fannie Brice, Eddie Cantor, Ed Wynn. . . .

Democracy opened all the doors that had been closed to them in the Old World. Yet even in the Golden Land there was often discrimination and anti-Semitism, remains of ignorance and hatred that lingered on. But they fought the evil with organizations, with protests, with mobilization of public opinion, with mass meetings, through educational channels, newspapers, pamphlets, radio, public addresses. America gave them the means for self-protection.

Living in freedom, the Jews were able to develop the life and culture of their own people in whatever part of the land they settled.

When the need for crowding into the older neighborhoods of the industrial cities disappeared, many of them moved out to the suburbs, where they could give their children air and light. Wherever they went, they created small communities, each with its synagogues and temples, its congregational schools and its Jewish Centers. Through the length and breadth of America they built seminaries, *Yeshivot,* and institutes for teachers. Thus America gradually became a Jewish cultural center. Less and less, as the years went by, did the Jews of America depend on the Old World for their scholarship. Scholarship became rooted in the New World, for the Jews built colleges, libraries, universities.

In the late part of the nineteenth century, Gratz College, dedicated to Jewish studies, was opened in Philadelphia. In 1909, close to Gratz College, Dropsie College for Hebrew and Cognate Languages was opened to Jews and Christians alike. In 1948, in Waltham, Massachusetts, a secular institution opened its doors, also to Jews and Christians. It was named in honor of the "people's lawyer," Brandeis University. They established private book concerns, and a publishing house called the Jewish Publication Society, which became the largest in the world, producing scholarly works, histories, children's books, an English translation of the Bible. In 1892 the American Jewish Historical Society was organized to collect and publish material on the history of the Jews in America and to encourage the study of Jewish history.

Yiddish had been the everyday language of the Jews of eastern Europe, the language of their newspapers, of many of their books and songs and poems. They did not want to lose their Yiddish culture in the new land where they had made their homes. So they built Yiddish schools for their children, and YIVO, the Yiddish Scientific Institute, to perpetuate the culture they had inherited from their fathers.

Many of their scholars came from the Old World, but did most of their work in the New. From the Old World came Max Margolis and Alexander Marx, historians, and Solomon Schechter, and Louis Ginzberg, scholars of the Jewish Theological Seminary, and Kaufman Kohler, a leader of Reform Judaism. Isaac Husik, who wrote on medieval Jewish philosophy, became a professor at the University of Pennsylvania, and Harry A. Wolfson, a professor at Harvard, contributed to the field of Jewish philosophy.

American Jewry had done its work well in the New World. It had shared in its building and in its development of the ideals of freedom. It had developed its own life, its teachers and leaders. It had planted the seeds of a rich culture in the Golden Land.

Things to Read

Leonard, Oscar, *Americans All,* "The Farmer's Friend," pp. 173-179; "He Fought Hunger," pp. 187-194; "He Was a Good Man," pp. 195-201; "She Lived on Henry Street," pp. 202-206; "The People's Advocate," pp. 207-215.
Pessin, Deborah, *Giants on the Earth,* "Saviour of Babies," pp. 110-114.

Questions to Discuss

Jewish history in America has been called a history without tears. Why? Compare the history of the Jews in America with their history in other lands.

Things to Do

Do a pageant on Jewish life in America from the beginning to the present day. Discuss thoroughly the ideas, the personalities, and the incidents you wish to highlight. You may want to present your pageant in the auditorium.

Write to the Institute for Democratic Education, 212 Fifth Avenue, New York 10, N.Y., for their recordings, "These Great Americans."

SKETCHES FROM

AMERICAN
JEWISH LIFE

Yankee Notions

On the Farm

Beyond the populated cities and towns of America lay the open spaces of the West, with towns rising along river banks and occasional farmhouses in the valleys and on the plains. Narrow roads wound through forestland, linking the cities with the farms. For months on end the roads were impassable. In the spring the wagons were bogged down in the mud. In the winter the roads disappeared under high blankets of snow or under crusts of ice. During the long winter months no one came to the farmhouses. They stood bleak and isolated in a white wilderness of snow.

The farmer puttered in his red barn, tending the chickens and cows, or in his tool shed, mending his plow. His wife worked in the kitchen, darning socks, cooking, baking. The children pressed their faces against the frozen window panes as they peered out over the white fields and the frozen forest.

Day by day the silence grew deeper. Soon the farmer's tools were mended. He moved restlessly about, looking for odd jobs to do. In the farmhouse, his wife sat peeling potatoes, an eye on the stove where her bread was baking. The children still pressed their faces against the windows, listening to the snow rustling along the sides of the house, watching the wind change the form of the snowdrifts.

Weeks went by, and still no one came to the farmer's door. He sat at the kitchen stove, reading last year's almanac. He wondered what his nearest neighbor, who lived ten miles away, was doing with himself. But there was no way to tell. His horse and wagon could never make it on the frosty road. He glanced over at his wife, who was stirring her pot of indigo. She looked peaked and worn. She had grown as silent and bleak as the wilderness stretching about them. A touch of sunshine was what she needed, thought the farmer, or a chat with someone outside her family. Clearing his throat, he asked whether she wanted some wood chopped. The children turned, startled at the sudden sound of his voice.

Gradually, the sharp winds died away. The air grew warmer. The icicles fell from the trees in the forest. Touches of brown showed through the melting snow. A robin came out of nowhere and settled on the red barn. The farmer, with boots reaching to his knees, stomped off to the tool shed. His wife, moving briskly, ironed the old kitchen curtains. The edges were frayed, she noticed with a frown. If only she had some material for new curtains. Now that spring was almost here, she would like some "Yankee notions" from the eastern cities, a pretty tea pot for her cupboard, some flowered calico, a bit of ribbon or lace for her bonnet. A touch of color rose in her pale cheeks as she hung the freshened curtains back on the windows.

The children, playing on the veranda of the house, gathered snow which they packed into hard balls, and hurled them toward the for-

est, making a game of seeing who could throw them the farthest. Suddenly, among the trees, they saw a moving form. They stood motionless on the veranda, watching the figure grow slowly larger as it came toward them. Then they opened their mouths and shouted, "The peddler!"

The Peddler

Their mother came hurrying from the house and their father from the barn. They all stood on the veranda, gazing at the figure bent under a huge load emerging slowly from the dark forest.

Soon the peddler stood before them, his face rosy, his eyes sparkling. The woman, who had not seen a strange face all winter, shyly asked him to come in, making fluttering movements with her hands. The farmer held the door open as the peddler, stooping so that his load would clear the top of the door jamb, entered the farmhouse, bringing with him the glow of the distant world.

The peddler rubbed his hands together to warm them as the farmer pulled up a chair for him beside the stove and his wife ran to fetch more firewood. The peddler sighed happily. It was good to rest, he said, settling back in his chair. He had come a long way, from the little settlement on the bank of the river at the opening of the forest trail.

Now the words began to flow. What news from the cities? Whom had he seen? The farmer lighted a pipe and offered one to the peddler. Would he like a glass of ale or a cup of tea? If only she had a pretty pot for her tea, thought the farmer's wife with a glance at the peddler's pack in the corner.

But the peddler was in no hurry to open his pack. He was happy to rest and talk for a while. His cheerful voice filled the kitchen, bringing to the farmer and his family the great world beyond the dark forest through which he had come. He told them about the cities he had visited, about the steamboats on the river, the machines in the factories, the omnibuses and stagecoaches in the cities, the covered wagons rolling farther and farther to the West. He told them about the lands across the sea, about the town in which he had lived, and where his movements had been restricted because he was a Jew. They listened spellbound, drinking in his anecdotes, his descriptions, his bits of news and gossip.

At last the peddler opened his pack. The children, who had been quietly watching him, standing quaintly in a row, now crowded around him. The farmer refilled his pipe. His wife leaned forward from her chair, her eyes sparkling as she watched the peddler pull his Yankee notions from his hundred-pound pack. There were bright new pots and pans, papers of pins, needles, rolls of ribbon and lace, small bags of tobacco, knives and forks and scissors, bolts of calico, a hand carved clock, some Irish linen. The farmer reached for a pipe and a small pocket knife. He turned the pipe over and

over in his hands, examining it carefully, as the peddler drew some red checkered gingham from his pack. The farmer's wife ran her work-worn hands over the pretty fabrics. Her face glowed with pleasure. The gingham would do up nicely as curtains, said the peddler, with a glance at the frayed curtains on the windows. He dug into his pack again and took out a white tea pot decorated with sprays of blue cornflowers. The farmer's wife gave a cry of delight as the peddler held out the pot for her to take. Again he dug into his pack, and this time pulled out a package tied with a red string. He winked at the awe-struck children, and they drew closer. When he had untied the string and drawn back the wrappings, they saw a heap of candy, shiny licorice and lemon zanzibars. To each child he gave a long strip of licorice and three lemon candies, and they withdrew to a corner of the room, crowing over their rich spoil. Back went the peddler to his pack, which seemed to be bottomless. Out came a new 1851 almanac, a six pound sugar loaf wrapped in purple paper, a box of factory-made nails, spools of colored thread, a packet of China tea.

At last they had seen all that the peddler had to offer. Carefully they made their choices—necessities for themselves and their home, a few pretty Yankee notions to cheer the farmer's wife, a new pipe, an almanac, a red ball for the children, some gingham for new curtains. The peddler re-assembled his stock and tied it in his pack. They pressed him to stay longer, but he said that he must go. He wanted to reach the next farmhouse before dusk. They waved to him from the veranda, watching him trudge up the slushy road. As he disappeared around a bend in the road, the farmer's wife sighed. Spring was here at last. The robin and the peddler had come.

At the Crossroads

Many peddlers, in time, saved up enough money to buy a horse and wagon. Sometimes a peddler's wagon was a grand affair, with sides that came down and double doors in the back that could open wide. On cold days, the peddler drove his wagon over icy roads, his knees covered with a buffalo skin and his feet perched on heated sandstone. When the peddler's wagon clattered into the farmyard, it was like a store rolling up to the farmer's door. The wagon held brooms, chairs, blankets, hats, boots, tea, chinaware, cloth, ribbon, lace, hardware, pewterware—almost everything the farmer might need for his home. Often the farmer's wife could not pay for some goods she needed. Then she would give the peddler something she no longer needed, but which he could sell, in exchange for the goods. Or if the farmer's wife had a pot with a hole in it, out came the pot when the peddler arrived, and he would earn a few pennies by mending it for her.

When roads began to develop, a peddler would often station his wagon at an important crossroads, instead of travelling from farm to farm. He ate and slept in his wagon, making it his home. When his supply of goods ran out, he went to the nearest large city, bought more goods, and returned to the crossroads. From hill and vale the farmers came to buy goods from the peddler at the cross-roads. If the crossroads trade was good, the peddler built a shack, and here he lived and sold his goods. In time he improved his shack, adding a few rooms, so that he had a real home in addition to a store.

More and more settlers came to the West. The store at the cross-roads grew. The roads became paved streets. The peddler, now turned storekeeper, added improvements to his store, a back room for storing large supplies of goods, a cubby hole for his desk, stool and books, rows of shelves to display his goods, a veranda in front of the store.

Several times a year large freight wagons drawn by teams of horses rolled up to the store at the crossroads. As the townspeople gathered round to watch, the drivers of the wagon and the store-keeper unloaded the city goods. There were barrels of vinegar, flour, hogsheads of molasses, rolls of lace, frying pans, buckshot, plows, scythes, coffee beans, tea, sugar loaves, sperm oil, candles, almanacs, bars of iron, kegs of wine, boots, hats, kegs of nails, dried fish, books, bolts of cloth, barrels of crackers, tools of all kinds, jewelry, clocks, brass goods. . . .

The store became the village center. Usually it was also the post office and the place where elections were held. Men dropped in at the store to chat and discuss the news. They sat around the pot-bellied stove on cold days, smoking their pipes and helping themselves to crackers from the open cracker barrel. On warm days they lounged on the veranda or played a game of horseshoes in the nearby field. On holidays, families got into their wagons and went to the busiest part of the neighborhood, the store. The children played out-of-doors. The men smoked their pipes and talked about their cattle and crops. The women examined the latest imports from the Yankee cities in the East.

Women often came to the store with butter, eggs or chickens which they exchanged for coffee, sugar, oil—whatever they happened to need. Men brought in pelts to trade for a plow or a scythe. If someone wanted a letter written, what better man to write it than the storekeeper, who had a jar of ink, a quill pen, and blotting sand. And most important, the storekeeper knew how to write. The storekeeper, who went to the city once or twice a year to buy goods, was a worldly figure to the country folk. He could tell them the latest political news. He could describe the big hotels with "Turkey rugs" on the floors. He could describe to the women the city styles, and he could sell them ribbons or feathers to make their bonnets look like the bonnets he had seen in the city stores.

The town continued to grow, and so did the country store. The storekeeper took in an assistant clerk to help him. He increased his stock, taking in more types of clothing, more imported and domestic goods, more Yankee notions. When railroad tracks were laid along the edge of the town, the trains brought the goods to the storekeeper.

For many years the store continued to be the center of the town, supplying its needs, keeping it abreast of the times, serving as the link between the East and the West.

Lower East Side
1885-1920

Side by side rise the tall, narrow brick buildings on Hester Street, Delancey Street, Orchard Street, Essex Street, Madison Street, Cherry Street, Pike Street, Houston Street, Henry Street, Pitt Street, Rivington Street. Here, in a small area of the lower East Side of New York City, hundreds of thousands of Jews from eastern Europe have made their homes.

Children play and shout on the crowded streets, tossing balls, rolling hoops, darting in and out among pushcarts and wagons. The streets are not simply places to walk through to the children of the lower East Side. They are extensions of their small, dark flats, and here they have more room to play in, more space to stretch their growing limbs. Above the shouts of the children are heard the cries of the ice man, the scissors and knife sharpener, the old clothes man. Men behind pushcarts also shout their wares.

"Fresh carp, white fish, flounder! Fish that melts like butter in the mouth. Come, women, buy!"

"Buy stockings, women, very cheap!"

"Apples, apples, who will buy?"

"Cabbage. Three cents a head. I'm giving it away for nothing. Three cents a head."

Women walk down the streets, from pushcart to pushcart, examining the goods. They also stop at the stands in front of the dim little stores. In the towns of Russia, the Jewish merchants used to

display their goods on stands, and they have brought the custom with them. Pushcarts and stands line the streets of the lower East Side.

Women who are not shopping and who have finished their housework lean from their windows, resting their arms on pillows they have put out to air. Sometimes they call across to a friend leaning from a window in a neighboring house.

"Has your husband found work yet?" Rebecca asks a friend sympathetically. She knows, from her friend's gloomy face, what the answer will be, but this is the way two women start a conversation on the lower East Side.

"Work!" her friend Miriam snorts. "Where does one find work these days? For every job there are ten workers ready to snatch it up. He trudges from shop to shop, but it's the same everywhere."

"It doesn't have to be in a clothing factory," Rebecca suggests. "Your Isaac is a willing worker. Let him turn his hand to something else."

"So I tell him," says Miriam hopelessly. " 'Isaac,' I plead with him, 'why should you wear out your feet looking for work? What pleasure do you get from sitting all day bent over a machine? Try something else, a little grocery store, a dry goods store, maybe a candy store.' But no!" And here a note of pride creeps into Miriam's voice. "He's a stubborn man, my Isaac. 'The streets are swarming with little stores,' he says. 'And do the storekeepers make a living? In a shop, a man can work himself up, perhaps even become a foreman.' "

"He'll find work," Rebecca consoles her neighbor. "Once the slack season is over, there will be work for everyone. In the meantime," she suggests, "perhaps I can lend you . . . perhaps. . . ."

But Miriam, who understands that her friend is offering to lend her money, interrupts quickly. "Thank God," she says, "we are not in need. My Samuel has a good job. Who would have thought of such work in the old country, making cigars? But in America everything is possible."

The friends are silent for a few minutes as they watch the scene below, the rows of pushcarts, the women with their shopping baskets, the horse-drawn wagons clattering along.

"My Samuel is a boy in a million," resumes Miriam, breaking the silence.

"A fine young man," Rebecca agrees.

"Tired as he is, he never misses his night school. Always with his nose in a book. Even at work, during the few minutes he has for lunch, his nose is in a book. 'Samuel,' I say to him, 'take a little time to breathe. Walk with a girl in the park. Go and see a movie.'

'That can wait,' my son says. 'First I'll become a teacher, then I'll walk with a girl in the park. America gives me permission to be a teacher, a doctor, whatever I like. Shall I be a cigarmaker all my life?' "

A ball comes flying up from the street and bounces on Rebecca's plump arm.

"You, Abie!" she shouts wrathfully to a boy on the sidewalk. "Take your ball and your friends and go somewhere else to play!"

As the ball comes hurtling down to earth again it lands on a pushcart filled with tomatoes and cucumbers. Abie quickly retrieves his ball and he and his friends take to their heels as the pushcart peddler examines his tomatoes for injuries.

"Boys," he mutters under his breath. "In the old country they were in *ḥeder,* learning how to be Jews. Here they run around like wild Indians."

The man at the next pushcart, a patriarchal figure with a white beard, has seen the accident and heard his neighbor's comments. He puts in a good word for the boys.

"They're only children," he says. "Where else can they play?"

"Did we play when we were children?" demands the first pushcart peddler angrily.

"You forget," says the old man. "We played different games, it is true, but we played. In America, they have other ways."

"America," sighs the first peddler, cutting up a damaged tomato and eating it. "They told us it was a golden land, where money grew in the streets." He looks up and down the crowded sidewalk and at the brick houses jammed together. "A golden land," he repeats bitterly.

"Would you return to the Czar, may his name be blotted out?" the white-bearded patriarch demands. "Do they have pogroms in America? Do they close the schools to your children because they are Jews?"

"If a man could only make a decent living," his neighbor sighs.

"A living!" retorts the patriarch. "You send your children to school. They will not be pushcart peddlers when they grow up. In America, a man reaches whatever heights he wishes, even a Congressman. What else do you want America to give you?"

The old man turns abruptly to a customer who has stopped at his pushcart.

"Dark brown shoe laces," says the customer.

"Dark brown," repeats the old man as he and the customer rummage through the stock—rolls of cheap lace and ribbon, safety pins, elastic, pencils, garters, eye-glasses, infants' shirts, handkerchiefs, an assortment of buttons. At last the old man picks up a pair of black shoe laces.

"Here," he says happily. "These are black, but who notices the color of shoe laces?"

"They must be dark brown," says the customer.

"I'll give them to you for less than they cost me, two cents."

"I need dark brown shoe laces," the customer insists. "I have a new pair of shoes and one of the laces broke. With an old pair it wouldn't matter." And turning away, he walks down the street in search of another peddler selling shoe laces.

The patriarch shrugs, indifferent to his loss, and from somewhere under his jumbled merchandise he draws out an old Hebrew book. Sitting down on a stool behind his pushcart, he opens his book and bends his head over the well-thumbed pages, oblivious to the shouts, cries, clatter of wagon wheels and jangling bells. Another customer comes along and tries on a pair of eye-glasses. The old man reads on, lost in his own world as the customer tries on one pair of glasses after another to see which are best suited to his eyes. The old man cares little about finding gold in the streets of America. If he brings home a dollar or two every day, he is satisfied with the herring and potatoes his wife sets before him. His children are married, able to take care of themselves, and the old man, who has never cared about worldly riches, is content with his humble way of life.

"Ole clothes! Ole clothes!" A wagon drawn by a skinny grey horse clatters down the street. On the wagon seat sits a man ringing a bell. "Ole clothes!" he cries. "Ole clothes!"

"Ole clothes! Ole clothes!" the children in the street mimic his cry. "Ole clothes! Ole clothes!"

The hubbub in the crowded street increases as the afternoon draws on toward evening. Women go from store to store, from push-cart to pushcart, to do their last-minute marketing. Some of the women have waited till late afternoon to shop, for the peddlers who have perishable goods are eager to get rid of them, and so they have lowered their prices. But for some women whose husbands hardly earn enough to feed the family, the prices are never low enough.

"How much is your flounder?" asks a woman wearing a faded shawl on her head.

"Ten cents a pound," says the fish peddler.

"Ten cents," the woman repeats. "Too much."

"If it is too much go and buy elsewhere," says the fish peddler.

"Here, I will give you twenty cents," the woman holds out two dimes temptingly. "Give me three pounds of fish. I have a large brood to feed."

"I have a large brood too," says the fish peddler. "At ten cents a pound I am almost giving it away."

The woman opens a little change purse, gropes around for a few moments, and finally takes out a five cent piece. She holds out her hand, revealing the nickel and the two dimes.

"Twenty-five cents," she says pleadingly. "That is all I can afford."

The fish peddler looks down at his fish and heaves a heavy sigh. He thinks of his own family, his wife and four young children. How is he to make ends meet if his profits are whittled down by those poorer than he is? Again he sighs, carefully weighs out three pounds of fish while the woman anxiously watches the scales, wraps the fish up in an old newspaper, and hands it over to his customer, who gives him her twenty-five cents. She tucks the package of fish safely into her shopping bag and hurries off to the bakery, where she hopes to buy a loaf of stale bread for five cents.

Down the street comes the watermelon man, selling thick slices of watermelon, a penny a slice.

"Cole watermelon! Cole watermelon!"

The children scatter into the tenement houses for pennies. They soon return, some with pennies clutched in their hands and some empty-handed. Those fortunate enough to have pennies run to the wagon where a man stands cutting a watermelon into slices. But suddenly a new cry echoes down the street.

"Ices! Ices!"

A man comes down the street wheeling a cart. He stops at the curb, where he has managed to find an empty space big enough for his cart, and scrapes ice from a large block. He puts the scraped ice into small paper cones and sprinkles the contents of each cone with whatever flavored syrup his customers demand—cherry, strawberry, orange, lemon, raspberry.

"Cole ices, ices!" shouts the ices man.

"Cole watermelon!" shouts the watermelon man.

As the afternoon deepens into shadows, the noises begin to subside. It has been a warm day, and now some of the women come out-of-doors with chairs which they set on the sidewalks in a row against the houses. They sit side by side, chatting as they breathe in the heavy evening air.

"Ole clothes! Ole clothes!"

The cry of the old clothes man fades in the distance as he makes his way home. The shrill hoot of a siren comes from a boat on the East River. Men and women are hurrying home now from shops and factories, folded newspapers under their arms. Some women, returning from work, stop to buy food on their way home, a loaf of bread at the bakery, a pound of meat at the butcher shop, perhaps some fish at the fish store on the corner. Girls sit on the stoops of their houses playing jacks. A boy darts up to a group of girls, snatches their ball, and races down the street, dodging in and out among the home-coming men and women. The girls race after him.

"Give us back our ball!" they scream.

A bigger boy stops the fleet-footed one.

"Give them back their ball. Boys don't start up with girls."

"Aw, leave me alone."

"I'm telling you, give them back their ball!"

The boy relinquishes the ball to the girls, who have gathered around, and the group scatters, each to his own affairs.

The streets are never empty on the lower East Side. People come home late from work, having remained at their shops to earn a few extra pennies. Men go to their little synagogues for evening prayer. Boys return from *heder,* Hebrew books under their arms. Pushcart peddlers wheel their pushcarts home. Men and women linger on the sidewalks to talk.

In the tenement flats the families sit in their kitchens, around tables covered with oilcloth. The lucky families have soup, meat, potatoes, bread, sometimes even a tomato or a cucumber. The poorer families eat herring and potatoes, or herring and bread.

"Benjy," a mother addresses her young son, "what did you learn in school today?"

Benjy learned arithmetic, spelling and geography.

"What is this geography?" his mother asks, her eyes resting fondly on her learned son.

"Where places are," Benjy explains carefully. "Like London is the capital city of England, and Paris is the capital city of France."

Benjy's mother beams.

"Already at his age he knows about England and France," she says proudly. And she predicts that Benjy will be a great man, a professor in a college.

Benjy's father, sipping a glass of hot tea, says it would be better for Benjy to be a doctor. Since people will always need doctors, Benjy will make a good living. Benjy's big brother Isidore, who works in a watch factory and goes to night school, says it is foolish to decide for Benjy what he will be. He will make up his mind when he grows up. But Benjy has already made up his mind. He will be a baseball player.

The tenement flats usually have three or four rooms. To help pay the rent, a family often takes in a boarder who occupies one of the bedrooms, if he has money to pay for it. If he is a poor boarder he sleeps on a folding bed in the kitchen, or in the "parlor," or "front room."

Miriam, whose husband has found no work that day, has been thinking of taking in a boarder. She waits till her son Samuel has gone off to night school before she broaches the subject. Isaac sits reading his Yiddish newspaper in the kitchen. It is spread open before him on the table. Eye-glasses are perched on his nose and his brow is furrowed as he reads an article on the American revolution. Isaac does not go to night school, but he learns many things about America from his Yiddish newspaper. Miriam takes out her darning and sits down at the table opposite her husband.

"Isaac," she begins hesitantly.

"Well?" He looks up at her from his newspaper, impatient at being interrupted.

"Maybe we ought to take in a boarder." All day she has been thinking how to say it tactfully, leading up to it step by step, but now that the moment has come she blurts it all out in one sentence. "It will help us with the rent," she goes on, "at least till you find work. The Axelrods have taken in a boarder, and they are five people in three rooms, and we are only three."

Isaac glares at his wife. "And where will you put a boarder?" he demands. "On the ceiling? Where will Sammy sleep?"

"Naturally Sammy will go on sleeping in the front room. But we can put a folding bed in the kitchen at night. We don't have to sit in the kitchen at night. We can sit in the front room till Sammy comes home. The Axelrods . . ."

Isaac slaps his hand down on the table. "I don't want to hear about the Axelrods. And if I want a glass of tea at night, while the boarder is asleep?"

Miriam sighs and threads a needle.

"Stop worrying," her husband says, his voice softening. "People don't starve in America. Have you gone hungry yet?"

It is a warm night, and people stroll up and down on the sidewalks or sit on chairs which they have carried out from their kitchens. The night schools in the neighborhood are filled. Every room is crowded with young people who work all day and come to study at night. Older people go to night school too. They do not expect to become doctors, teachers or lawyers, like their children, but they want to learn English, and how to become "real Americans." They want to find out who Abraham Lincoln was, and how one votes in America. There was no voting in the old country. There was a Czar, and there was nothing anybody could do about it.

Meyer and Eva are both studying English together in night school. They live in the same tenement house, and now they are walking home. As they stroll along they discuss their plans. Meyer will be a doctor some day. He and Eva will get married and move away from the lower East Side, to some place where there is more air to breathe. Perhaps they will move to Brooklyn, or to another city. It takes many years of studying before one can be a doctor, but Meyer is only eighteeen. He will save as much money as he can to go to medical school. Eva, who is seventeen, says she will wait for him.

There are few saloons or bars on the lower East Side. There are coffee houses instead. Men sit around the little tables of the coffee houses for hours, talking and arguing and discussing. They discuss politics, shop work, unions, how to get rich, the Yiddish theatre on Second Avenue, the stories of their favorite writer, Sholom Aleichem.

The night wears on. The hum of sewing machines comes from open windows. People linger on stoops to catch a breath of fresh air before they retire to their hot bedrooms. Some people drag their mattresses up to the roof, where they will spend the night, hoping that there will be a breeze from the East River. Folding beds come out in kitchens and "front rooms." Benjy, asleep beside his big brother, dreams that he has hit a home run and the whole lower East Side is shouting its approval as the ball goes sailing over the house-tops. Eva, ironing a white blouse to wear to the factory the next morning, wonders how many years it will take Meyer to become a doctor. The patriarchal old pushcart peddler closes his book and prepares to go to bed, humming an old Hebrew melody.

"Sammy," Miriam calls from her bedroom, "stop reading and go to sleep. Tomorrow is another day."

Dawn breaks gently over the streets of stone and brick, tinting them with soft, pale light. Slowly stores and houses come to life. Children dart out of the dark doorways and run to the grocery stores to buy milk and rolls for breakfast. The smell of coffee wafts out of open windows. Doors creak and pans rattle. Soon the houses are being emptied of their multitudes, the children streaming to school, the men and women to factories and shops. Storekeepers bring out their stands and set them up in front of their stores, and pushcart peddlers arrange their stock on their pushcarts at the curbs of the streets. Thousands of America's pioneers are starting a new day.

Jewish Community, U.S.A.

At the Beginning

The Jewish community we are visiting is in the midwest, not too far from a river, not too far from the prairies through which the covered wagons rolled during the Gold Rush to the West. Our community is in a good-sized city, but the buildings are not tall enough to shut out the sky, and on warm nights a cool wind comes in from the river. Once Judah Touro's boats sailed up the river from New Orleans, loaded with goods for points north, and boys like Huckleberry Finn, fishing along its banks, watched the boats lazily as their lines dangled in the water. Before the coming of the white man, only Indians knew the mighty river, and their canoes skimmed over its shining waters like swift eels, bending with the wind, following every curve in its long course. Then the white man came from the East, pushing back the frontier, setting up stockades and cabins on the river bank. Farther and farther inland the Indians went, leaving the river and the forests and the plains for the white man and his descendants.

We do not know just when the first Jewish settlers came to our Jewish community. But there is an old Jewish graveyard at the outskirts of the city, a small graveyard at the foot of a hill, guarded by giant oaks and a hoary weeping willow. The few stones are half sunken in the ground and the inscriptions are all but obliterated. On one of the tombstones are words barely legible: Samuel Frankfurter, and the dates, 1786–1856. And a few Hebrew words:

Zikhrono Livrakha, May His Memory Be Blessed. Frankfurter is a German name, so we assume that Samuel came from Germany, from the ghetto of the city of Frankfurt on the Main. Was Samuel a peddler, carrying a pack of Yankee notions on his back, then setting up a small store in the settlement near the river?

So his great-great-grandson, Edward Franks, who has a small but well-stocked department store on Main Street, tells us. People often changed their names in America, leaving off syllables, altering the spelling. Edward Franks, who belongs to a Reform temple and is a member of B'nai B'rith, can tell you more about name changing, more about the different nationalities that make up his city, than anyone else in town. Mr. Franks made a special study of the subject for a talk he had to give. It happened this way. One night several years ago, some hoodlums smashed the window of his store. Attached to the rock they threw at the window was a note saying that America belonged to Christians only. Quite a number of people were upset by the incident. They didn't like that kind of thing happening in their city. They thought that America was through with prejudice and violence. It happened that Brotherhood Week, arranged by the National Conference of Christians and Jews, was approaching. The National Conference invited Edward Franks to give a talk called, "Beginnings of Our City." This was to be their answer to the hoodlums, showing that America was built by immigrant pioneers, and that these pioneers came from every part of the world and practiced every religion imaginable, including a number of religions the hoodlums had never heard of. The police, of course, had their own way of dealing with the hoodlums. Edward Franks' talk took several weeks of preliminary work. He did some careful research at the university, getting the help of two professors of history who became quite excited about the subject. Their search led them to old graveyards, to the historical society, to the records kept in City Hall, to societies of Irishmen, Italians, Swedes, Norwegians, Armenians, Frenchmen. . . . The societies all had records of their own first pioneers, and they were happy to cooperate. Edward Franks' talk proved what it was expected to prove, that America belonged to everyone, and it was printed in one of the city newspapers.

Cultural Pluralism

It does not matter to Jacob Katz, aged thirteen, nor to his Italian friend, Antonio Morello, whether their ancestors came to America first or somewhere in the middle or last, on the fastest steamer in the world. The ancestors of both boys came because they wanted a better life in America. Jacob and Antonio belong to the same scout troop, go to the same public school, belong to the same baseball team, the Wildcats. But there are some places they belong to separately. Tony and his parents attend a Catholic church and Tony goes to the church Sunday school. Jacob's parents belong to one of the Conservative congregations, and Jacob and his sister Dinah attend the congregational school attached to it.

Jacob and Tony are tossing a ball back and forth on a lazy afternoon in spring. They stand on the tree-shaded sidewalk in front of Jacob's house, and the ball goes smack into Tony's glove.

"Good pitch, Jake," says Tony. He tosses back the ball, a low curve, then asks, "What's that your mother's cooking? I can smell it all the way out here."

"Fish," says Jacob.

"Don't kid me," says Tony. "Fish doesn't smell that good."

"Special kind of fish we eat on the Sabbath, tonight. *Gefilte* fish."

"This is Friday. I thought your Sabbath was tomorrow."

"It starts Friday evening. Say, why don't you eat with us tonight? Then you'll know what *gefilte* fish tastes like. And you can hear *Kiddush* and everything."

"You bet!" says Tony. And he jams the ball into his pocket and starts down the street for home.

"Say, what are you going home for?"

"To take a bath and put on my Sunday clothes. It's your Sabbath, isn't it?"

After Tony has dined with Jacob's family that night, he takes home a few pieces of *gefilte* fish for his own family, with some *ḥalah*, the Sabbath bread, to go with it. When Tony's mother calls several days later to get the recipe for the fish, she gives Mrs. Katz a recipe she learned from her mother in Italy for spaghetti and meatballs.

The boys may never have heard the term, nor their mothers either, for that matter, but this is what we call "cultural pluralism," cultures living side by side, respecting one another and learning from one another. We see examples of cultural pluralism all around us, when a church and a synagogue stand on the same street, when the Irish march on St. Patrick's Day, when people go to the park mall in their national costumes and dance their national dances, when the teacher in public school asks a Jewish pupil to tell the class about Ḥanukah and why it is celebrated, when children at camp sing Negro spirituals. All this is cultural pluralism. It is the American way of life.

Synagogues and Schools

There are about five thousand Jews in our community. Old men, young men, old women, young women, boys, girls, babies. Looking at them, you could never tell where they or their fathers or ancestors came from. They are light-skinned, dark-skinned, blue-eyed, black-eyed, brown-eyed, grey-eyed, light-haired, dark-haired, tall, short, medium, slender, stocky. It's a myth, of course, that all Jews have black hair and dark eyes. One's coloring depends a good deal on the place he lives in, on geographical factors, that is.

Our five thousand Jews have synagogues, because there are synagogues wherever Jews live. Naturally, there was no synagogue for Samuel Frankfurter, the pioneer who died in 1856, when he arrived at the little frontier settlement. He probably waited impatiently for the day when more of his co-religionists would join him. It must have been lonely, praying all alone, away from family and friends, wondering who would care for him if he were ill, see to it that he got *kosher* food to eat. We hope he did not have too long to wait before he could reach out his hand and cry, *"Shalom Aleikhem!"* to the next Jew who made the long trek from the Old World to the settlement on the bank of the river.

But the days of waiting are over. The Jews are five thousand strong, and their numbers increase as the population of the city increases. Our community now has two Orthodox synagogues, one Conservative synagogue, and one Reform temple. And attached to the synagogues and temple there are Jewish schools. There is a Yiddishist school besides, where children are taught Yiddish, and there are recreational facilities and adult classes at the Jewish Center.

The schools are lively places, all of them. The children study Hebrew, Jewish history, Jewish current events, and the songs and prayers of their people. The advanced classes also study the Bible in the original. The children do art work besides, and dancing and dramatic work. On the Sabbath, they have their own services in the school auditorium. And of course, they celebrate their festivals with plays, pageants, masquerades.

Michael Greenberg, a boy in an advanced class, once brought his grandfather, Solomon Greenberg, to Hebrew school with him. The old, white-haired gentleman was given a seat of honor in front of the room, near Miss Levinson's desk. He listened intently as the children conversed in Hebrew with their teacher. He raised his eyebrows in amazement as one of them read a Hebrew story he had written the night before. His brows rose higher as he heard the class discuss the development of the Talmud.

"Well!" he breathed at last. "Times have certainly changed."

"From when, sir?" asked Miss Levinson.

"From when I was a boy," said Mr. Greenberg. And to the delight of Miss Levinson and the children, he began to tell them about the days when he was a boy.

Looking Back

"My family came from Russia," began Mr. Greenberg, "from Grodno, and went straight to the lower East Side of New York. You never saw such a place. The crowds, the smells, the pushcarts. I thought that all of America was crowded into the few streets of the East Side. We were packed into a three-room flat, my parents, my three sisters, and I. At one time, when my father was out of work, we even had a boarder. I don't remember where he slept. Probably in the kitchen.

"I went to a *ḥeder,* of course, because there was nothing better. The *ḥeder* was in the kitchen of the *rebbe's* flat, so dark that it was lit by gaslight all day, and smelling of the food his wife cooked while we—there were five of us—learned to read Hebrew and recite the prayers. He had a peppery beard, our *rebbe,* black streaked with white and grey, and a peppery temper too. When he suspected that one of the boys wasn't paying attention, off came his strap. Of course, I felt that strap more than once. And he didn't know much, our *rebbe.* They say he started as a peddler, couldn't make a living at it, and decided to have a *ḥeder* instead. He couldn't have made much of a living at that either.

"Anyway, my father, who was a miller in the old country, accustomed to the open air, couldn't stand the sweatshop he worked in. He began to develop pains in the chest. My mother got scared and insisted that we move. 'What do we have to lose?' she pleaded with my father. 'The sweatshop? America is big. Why do we have to crowd into the East Side like sardines?' So we came out here, because my mother had a brother here, and he could help us get started.

"There were three synagogues and one Reform temple when we came to this city. The Reform temple was fairly new, a good, strong, brick building. One of the synagogues was in a rented wooden building on Elm Street. The other was a converted church, also made of wood, from which its original owners had moved to larger quarters. The third was a converted blacksmith shop. It stood on the spot where the post office now stands."

"That's right," said Ben Silver. "There's a plaque there, on a post in front of the post office, saying that it's the site of the first synagogue in the city."

Mr. Greenberg nodded. "The building was pulled down," he said, "when I was still a boy. I remember it had long wooden benches and a raised platform for the pulpit. They're all gone now, the old synagogues. Bigger ones took their place because the Jews kept coming. It's a good town. My father got his strength back and lived to a ripe old age."

The old man stopped for a few moments as he looked back into the past at his childhood.

"Anyway," he went on, "the synagogue in the wooden building —it had once been a private residence—had several rooms. And one of these rooms was a *ḥeder*. That's where I went. But it wasn't much better than the *ḥeder* in New York. The *rebbe* wasn't peppery. He was sleepy, always dozing off. As soon as he began to doze, out came our pocket knives and bits of wood to carve and our sling shots and whatever else we carried in our pockets. Suddenly, when we were in the midst of doing something important, our *rebbe* would wake up with a start and slap his hand down on the table and scold us for wasting our time. Now, you mustn't think all the *rebbes* were like that. There were some very good ones, real students of the Bible and Talmud. But I didn't have any luck with mine. You children are lucky."

And here he turned to Miss Levinson and his eyes twinkled as he bowed gallantly in her direction. The class laughed, and Miss Levinson laughed too.

"Why did you go to that kind of a *heder?*" asked Becky Fisher when the laughter had died down.

Mr. Greenberg looked at Becky in astonishment. "That was the only kind of Jewish school we had. So naturally, that's where I went. But I understand we were better off than the generation before us." He turned to Miss Levinson again. "There were no schools at all then, were there?"

"That's right," said Miss Levinson. "There were some Jewish day schools, but they were in the larger cities. And, of course, there were no public schools, either."

"No public schools!" cried Mr. Greenberg. He had taken it for granted that there had always been public schools in America.

"There were parochial schools belonging to the churches," Miss Levinson told him. "Jewish children went there to study reading, writing and arithmetic. Many Jewish parents were concerned about it. They were afraid their children might drift away from their own people. But after the Civil War the idea of the public school began to spread."

"And a good thing," said Mr. Greenberg with satisfaction. "Now in the old country . . ."

And Mr. Greenberg went on telling them about the old country till the bell rang and it was time to go home.

Palestine

Sometimes the schools and synagogues get together for some special celebration, like the one in 1948 when Israel declared itself an independent state. It was a lively time in our Jewish community when the news flashed out over the world. Women picked up their telephones and called their husbands at the offices, in case they hadn't heard. Some of the people cried. Some began to make plans to visit Israel to see what it was like. Feverish preparations began at the Hebrew schools to celebrate the rebirth of Israel. Even the kindergarten children were excited, although they didn't quite understand what the excitement was about.

Rabbi Friedman, of a Reform temple, telephoned to Rabbi Levine, of a Conservative synagogue, and suggested that the schools get together for the celebration. The idea caught on, and it was decided that all the schools, Conservative, Reform, Orthodox and Yiddishist, hold one mass celebration. Mr. Handler, who is a writer, got together with the teachers of the schools to plan a pageant called, "The Dream Came True." Mr. Marcus, a cantor, offered to coordinate the music. The art-craft teachers worked with costumes and stage sets. Mr. Berger, director of the Jewish Center, offered the Center auditorium for the celebration. But Dr. Wilkens, principal of Central High School, offered his school auditorium which is the largest in town.

On the day of the celebration the auditorium was packed. Jacob Katz brought his friend Tony, and everybody else's good friends, Jews and Gentiles, were there too. Dr. Wilkens, who came with his wife and children, looked out at the crowd and remarked to Rabbi Kraus that it was like the Israelite encampment at Mount Sinai. Rabbi Kraus said, "Yes, except that now they have reached the Promised Land." They had to put up two loud speakers so that those who couldn't get in and had to sprawl on the lawn could at least hear what was being said.

After two rabbis spoke, the Reverend Mr. Shields, Presbyterian, also gave a talk, based on a quotation from Isaiah that a remnant of Israel would return to Palestine. A representative of Hadassah, the Women's Zionist Organization, followed Mr. Shields. She spoke about Hadassah and its work in Palestine. Mrs. Hendricks told her audience about Henrietta Szold, how she visited Palestine, how grieved she had been when she saw the ravages of time, the ruins and the disease, how she came back to America and founded

Hadassah, how it grew and grew, with branches all over the country, and how it brought health to Palestine—nurses, hospitals, doctors, health centers, clinics.

Then Mr. Davidson, a member of the Zionist Organization of America, was called upon. He said he would make his talk short because the children would grow restless. But naturally, it turned out to be long, since he had so much to say. Mr. Davidson told about the early Zionist societies of the Russian Jews. He spoke about Theodor Herzl, the Viennese journalist stationed in Paris who dreamed of gathering his people from the lands of their dispersion and bringing them back to their ancient homeland. Mr.

Davidson described the World Zionist Organization, which Herzl founded, and the Zionist Organization of America and its work in Palestine.

After Mr. Davidson's talk it was time for the pageant. This was the most interesting part of the celebration. "The Dream Came True" moved smoothly along, holding the audience spellbound. Scene followed scene without a break, merely by shifting the spotlight from one part of the stage to another. First the light picked out a short, swift scene in Russia, a pogrom, done in stark pantomime, with the announcer explaining briefly what was happening. Then came an old Jewish patriarch in a synagogue, alone, his head lifted in prayer, his voice filled with agony as he chanted the old Hebrew prayer, *Aheinu Kol Bet Yisrael.* . . . May the Lord have mercy on our suffering brethren, whether they are on the land or on the sea. . . . May He bring them out of darkness into light. . . . The scenes flowed into each other, the exodus from the villages of the Pale, a group of *halutzim,* pioneers, working in Palestine, Theodor Herzl addressing a Zionist Congress, Henrietta Szold addressing a small group of women. . . . On and on it went, while the audience sat motionless, watching the children give the story of the rebirth of Israel. When it was over, the audience rose to its feet, applauding wildly, shouting for encores of some of the songs.

Federation

When Peter Stuyvesant met the group of twenty-three Jews who came to New Amsterdam from Brazil, he wrote to the Dutch West India Company complaining that they were poor. The Dutch West India Company replied that they could stay anyway, provided they took care of their own poor. Had Asser Levy read the letter, he would have laughed. The Dutch West India Company could not have known much about the Jews and their customs. They did not know, for example, that the farmers in ancient Israel left a corner of their fields for the poor, and that any sheaves of wheat that fell from the hands of the gleaner were left to lie in the field for the poor, and that Jews had always ransomed Jewish captives, and taxed themselves so that the poor would be taken care of. It was needless for the directors of the Dutch West India Company to put in the condition for their remaining in New Amsterdam. But of course, they did not know.

This taking care of the poor in America began with the little group of twenty-three and went right on, with other little groups, with congregations, with the *landsmanschaften,* with the societies, with the ladies auxiliaries connected with the synagogues, with the branches of B'nai B'rith and other lodges and fraternal organizations.

Let us take leave of our community for a little while and go back to the year 1870, when the city was still very young. The Sinai Lodge of the B'nai B'rith is holding a meeting. The men are arranging for visits to one of their sick members. The secretary is making a list of who does the visiting, and when the visits are to be. Doctors and nurses are scarce, and the sick man's wife would soon be sick too if she had no help. The lodge members want to be sure the sick man is not left alone for a minute. The "night watch" is very important, so they arrange for two members to visit him from 7 P.M. to 1 A.M., and two from 1 A.M. to 7 A.M. If someone fails in his duty and does not show up, he is to be fined. If he sends a substitute to take his place, he is also fined.

Now that this is arranged, they talk of other things. They plan a picnic with their families, or a boat ride. Someone mentions the yellow fever epidemic out in Tennessee. They decide to send one hundred dollars to help the victims. Someone asks how much they have in their widows' fund. Six thousand dollars, a good sum. It is too bad that the directors of the Dutch West India Company could not have been present at one of those Sinai Lodge meetings, or at the meeting of a synagogue, or of a *landsmanschaft*.

As the number of Jews in our community increased, their needs and organizations grew more numerous. After a while things got rather complicated. The people of our community began to lose track of what they were contributing for, since they were called upon to contribute so often, for coal, for *matzah,* for helping a new family that had just arrived, for a hospital, for a home for old people. . . . "Why not combine our charities," they asked, "as Jews are doing in other cities? Why not contribute a large sum to one central organization which will take care of all our needs?"

Thus, after much trial and error, arose the United Jewish Charities, later changing its name to Federation. And now it is Federation, with a trained, efficient staff and with many different departments that takes care of all the particular needs that arise in our community—hospitals, orphanages, Jewish Centers and schools. . . . Every year Federation runs its drive for money, and every year the people contribute whatever sum they can, knowing that things will be taken care of efficiently. Some of the needs are complicated, but Federation is prepared to handle them.

Mrs. Einhorn, for example, comes to the offices of Federation with a problem. Her husband is ill. She does not want to accept money from anyone. She would like to go out to work, but there is no one to take care of her children. What is she to do?

Federation turns Mrs. Einhorn's case over to the Social Service Bureau. Mrs. Einhorn meets a pleasant young woman, Miss Ellis, who listens carefully to her story. Then Miss Ellis visits Mrs. Einhorn at her home. The home is in the poorer section of the city, and there are three children, the oldest only six. Mr. Einhorn, a glazier, has had a bad accident and will not be on his feet for six months. He has already been at home for three months. Most of their savings are gone, used for food, rent and doctor bills.

Miss Ellis sees that the family needs help at once. Mr. Einhorn is upset at the idea of taking money from Federation. His wife is upset at the idea of leaving him and the children to go out to work. Besides, she would have to pay someone to take care of them while she is away working. They pour out their troubles and look at Miss Ellis anxiously, wondering what she will suggest.

Miss Ellis sees a way out. It would obviously not be very sensible to let Mrs. Einhorn go to work when her husband and children need her at home. Mr. Einhorn makes a good salary when he is at work. All they really need is a loan. Miss Ellis suggests that Mrs. Einhorn remain at home and that Mr. Einhorn accept a loan from the Free Loan Society affiliated with Federation. When he is at work again, he will repay the money in small sums, so that the family will not feel deprived.

Mr. and Mrs. Einhorn breathe a sigh of relief. Their troubles are over.

Help Overseas

The same is true of help overseas in our Jewish community. The greater and more complex the needs, the more efficient became the community in handling them. And the needs were very great during the two world wars.

It was a trying time for our community, as it was for everybody else in the city, when the United States entered the First World War. People kept buying the latest editions of every newspaper, looking through the lists of casualties, hoping that the names of their boys were not on the lists. But names did come through, as happens in every war. At the end of the war they put up a memorial column in Richter Park, the park that was presented to the city by Morris Richter, a Jewish Congressman, in memory of his son Charles who was killed in battle in France. On the column were engraved the names of the boys killed in action—Michael Kilroy, Joseph Cohen, Leonard Costello, James Stevenson, Amos Levine, Stephen Parrish, Charles Richter, Richard Andrews. . . . Jews and Gentiles, they all died together for the country that was home.

But that came after the war. As the battles raged in Europe, the Jews in our community had not only their own boys to worry about. They worried about their people on the Eastern Front caught between the two warring armies, the Russians and the Germans. Bit by bit details kept coming through in the American newspapers. Our community read about Jews wandering through forests, homeless and hungry. They read about towns wiped out. People looked for names of relatives whom they had left behind in the old country. *Landsmanschaften* kept sending money for food, clothes, shelter. Everybody tried to do something, but there was no organization. There were plenty of committees, but no central body to organize the work of the committees.

Finally, when the Joint Distribution Committee was set up, our community began to work more effectively. Two million dollars was collected for JDC. Priests and ministers made appeals in their churches. Rabbis and other Jewish leaders addressed large meetings. Children emptied their piggy banks. When the war ended, money kept pouring into the treasury of the JDC to help the work of reconstruction.

Years passed in Jewish Community, U. S. A. The boys who were soldiers had returned. They had married, and now it was their children who played in the back yards and on the tree-shaded sidewalks, who went fishing in the river and berry picking in the forest. Then the children grew up and went to high schools, colleges and universities. A new Jewish Center was built on Wood Street, with classrooms, a swimming pool, showers, and an auditorium. Things rolled smoothly along, people working, building, getting together of an evening, holding meetings, hearing concerts, talking about their children and gardens.

Then came another, the Second World War, fiercer, deadlier, than the first. This time there was Adolf Hitler, who wiped out six million Jews, the largest Jewish community in the world. All that the Jews of our city could do, besides following the nightmare stories in the newspapers and sending their boys to fight, was to help those of their people overseas who were left, those who managed to reach Palestine. So they poured money into Palestine itself, helping to make it a homeland for the remnant that had remained alive. Zionists and non-Zionists in our community worked shoulder to shoulder to help bring about the rebirth of Israel.

Harvest

The wars are over as we walk the quiet streets of our mid-western city. A wind blows in from the river, stirring the leaves on the elms and the maple trees. It is evening, and lights go on here and there in the houses along the streets. Music from radios wafts from the open windows. And now and then a voice.

"Do your homework, Henry."

"What's for dinner, mom? I'm hungry."

"Did you have a good day at the office?"

Jewish Community, U. S. A., is relaxing after a day's work. The doctors, dentists, mechanics, lawyers, glaziers, teachers, carpenters, salesmen, engineers, painters, storekeepers, are sitting in their easy chairs, glancing through their evening newspapers.

"Did you read this, Ruth? Varsity beat State University, eight to six."

They are part of the larger community around them, just as they are part of their own smaller community. They have the same interests as their Christian neighbors, the same obligations. They contribute to the Community Chest as well as to their own Federation. Samuel Nelson, a successful business man, does not limit his gifts to his own people. He likes children, so he presented the scout organization with a gift, a camp on a lake, twenty miles from the city.

As we walk down the street we pass the Home for the Aged, set on a wide green lawn. The old people sit on benches under the trees, enjoying the cool evening air. The wind rises from the river, and a white-haired woman pulls her shawl closer around her shoulders.

"My son and his wife came to see me today," she tells her friend. "They want me to live with them."

"Why should you live with them?" her friend asks.

"That's what I say. Here I do as I please. A doctor and nurses to look after me. When I want to see them, I go to see them, my son and his family."

Since Federation took over, the Jewish Home for the Aged is not what it used to be. They built a new home, with bright sunny rooms, with gardens for the old men to putter in, with a recreation room where they can play checkers and chess on a rainy afternoon.

There are lights on the river and along the shoreline. The skies grow darker. But the city does not sleep. Dr. Greenbaum hurries off to a meeting of his Medical Association. The brotherhood of the B'nai Zion Congregation is meeting to discuss its budget for the coming year. The Jewish Center is having a dance for young people in its gymnasium. Mr. Roth is going to a meeting of his B'nai B'rith lodge. His wife is also going to a meeting. She is on the Planning Committee of the PTA of the Charles Street Public School. Jacob Katz is telephoning his friend Tony. He lost his homework assignment. Mrs. Klein is sewing a costume for her daughter, who is in a Hebrew school play. Mr. Greenberg is reading his Yiddish newspaper which comes to him once a week from New York. Sarah Simons is writing her boy friend at State University a letter.

The night wears on. The lights go out, even the lights on the river. The city sleeps. Only Rabbi Kraus is awake. He is sitting in his study, preparing his weekly sermon. It will deal with the life of happiness and security the Jews have built in America after the centuries of bitter oppression they suffered in the Old World. Rabbi Kraus decides that he will take the text for his sermon from Psalm 126: "They that sow in tears shall reap in joy."

INDEX

311